The Light *of* Dawn

God is the Light of the heavens and the earth.
The parable of His light is,
as it were, that of a niche containing a lamp;
the lamp is enclosed in glass, the glass like a radiant star;
lit from a blessed tree—an olive-tree
that is neither of the east nor of the west—
the oil of which would almost give light
even though fire had not touched it: light upon light!
God guides to His light the one who wills to be guided;
and God offers parables to human beings,
since God has full knowledge of all things.

[24:35]

(translation of cover calligraphy)

A SHAMBHALA THRESHOLD BOOK

OTHER BOOKS BY CAMILLE ADAMS HELMINSKI

Rumi Daylight: A Daybook of Spiritual Guidance,
Mevlâna Jalâluddin Rumi.
Translated by Camille and Kabir Helminski, 1999.

Jewels of Remembrance: A Daybook of Spiritual Guidance,
Mevlâna Jalâluddin Rumi.
Selected and translated by Camille and Kabir Helminski, 2000.

Awakened Dreams, Ahmet Hilmi.
Translated by Refik Algan and Camille Helminski, 1993.

Happiness Without Death, Desert Hymns, Assad Ali.
Translated by Camille and Kabir Helminski
and Dr. Ibrahim Al-Shihabi, 1991.

The Light of Dawn

Daily Readings from the Holy Qur'ān

Selected and rendered by

CAMILLE ADAMS HELMINSKI

SHAMBHALA

Boston & London

2000

SHAMBHALA PUBLICATIONS, INC.
Horticultural Hall
300 Massachusetts Avenue
Boston, Massachusetts 02115
www.shambhala.com

9 8 7 6 5 4 3 2 1

FIRST SHAMBHALA EDITION
Printed in the United States of America

⊚ This edition is printed on acid-free paper that meets the
American National Standards Institute Z39.48 Standard.
Distributed in the United States by Random House, Inc.,
and in Canada by Random House of Canada Ltd

LIBRARY OF CONGRESS CATALOGING-IN-PUBLICATION DATA
Koran. English & Arabic. Selections
The light of dawn : daily readings from the holy Qur'an /
selected and rendered by Camille Adams Helminski.
p. cm.
Originally published under slightly different subtitle:
Brattleboro, Vt. : Threshold Books, 1998.
ISBN 1–57062–597–2 (pbk.)
I. Helminski, Camille Adams, 1951– . II. Title
BP110 2000
297 .1'22521 – dc21   00–040034
                                        CIP

Contents

*Dedicated
to the Sun of Reality
and all those who open to Its Light*

*It is God Who sends to His servants clear signs
that He may lead you out of the depths of darkness
into the Light.
And truly, God is to you Most Kind and Merciful.*

[*Surah al-Hadid*, 57:9]

Preface:

The Light of Dawn

Bismillāhir Raḥmānir Raḥeem

Not long ago, though it happened almost 1400 years before these days in chronological time, someone's heart opened: a man named Muhammad, the trustworthy, received the Word of God. Such a power the delivery of this Word effected upon him that he felt as though his ribs were almost crushed in the Angel Gabriel's embrace. The command "Read!" shook him to the bone. He felt his incapacity, and responded, "But I cannot."[1] Gabriel repeated the command of His Lord:

> *"Recite!" In the name of Your Sustainer Who created,*
> *created humankind from a connecting cell:*
> *"Recite!" And your Sustainer is the Most Generous,*
> *He Who taught by the pen,*
> *taught humankind what it did not know!*[2]

The Word burst forth as such a compelling light within the heart of Muhammad that it had to be shared as a *guidance and a mercy to all humankind.*[3] For twenty-three years Muhammad (Peace and Blessings upon Him) was the faithful receptor of His Lord's Word— from the age of forty until shortly before his death at age sixty-three.

---

[1] Muhammad's words were, *"Maa ana bi Qaari."* ("I am not a reciter." or " I am not one who reads.")

[2] Qurʾān: *Surah ʾIqraʾ*, 96:1-5.

[3] Qurʾān: *Surah Yūnis*, 10:57.

Truly our Sustainer is gracious and pours down abundant sustenance time after time, era by era, moment by moment. Gratitude opens the floodgates of abundance wider still. True gratitude manifests as charity to His creation—how can we not share of that sustenance which is bestowed upon us? As Muhammad was compelled to share of the sustenance that was given to him, little by little, others opened to receive nourishment from the Word, the guidance which he conveyed.

Now, centuries later, millions of people continue to find a life-renewing Light within the words of the Qur'ān, the recitation received by Muhammad. The Prophet understood from the verses of the Qur'ān itself that the message he was conveying was the same Word received by Abraham, by Moses, and by Jesus; that his role was as a reminder, a warner, confirming the Truth of earlier revelations.

Some time ago, the Light began to dawn for me that great Truth was contained within the Qur'ān. First through the verses of Mevlana Jalaluddin Rumi which elucidated phrases of the Qur'ān and then, slowly, from the Qur'ān itself. I came to understand and witness the universes of meaning that can open from a single *ayah* or "sign" which the word used to designate a verse of the Qur'ān also means.

Listen then to Me; pay heed, pay attention is a continually repeated refrain within the Qur'ān. Witness the unfolding of meaning within yourself and upon the farthest extension of the horizon of creation.[4] If we look, how can we not witness the beauty and magnificence of this creation—and who could have made it, but our Sustainer—the Unknowable and Infinite and Sublimely Skillful and Beneficent Source of Being? Surely it was

---

[4] Qur'ān: *Surah Fuṣṣilat*, 41:53

not man that made it thus—*in shapely proportion*[5] and *without any flaw.*[6]

A daily opening to the light of God made manifest as Word cannot but help to guide our lives into a better groove. The Qur'ān calls it the "straight path." Why waste time, especially when we can never know how much time we have. Each moment could be precious. How will we know unless we taste of its nectar, unless we open to its possibility?

As Mevlana Jalaluddin Rumi says,

> Open a window towards God
> and begin to delight yourself
> by gazing upon Him through the opening.
> The business of love is to make this window in the heart,
> for the breast is illumined by the beauty of the Beloved.
> Gaze incessantly on the face of the Beloved.
> Listen, this is in your power, my friend.

> [*Mathnawi* IV, 3095-3097]

Within these pages are a selection of verses from the Holy Qur'ān as it was revealed to Muhammad when the window of his heart was opened wide to his Lord. The power of these words has not diminished. Sound by sound, the words draw one into the Heart of creation, into the Beneficence of an Infinitely Compassionate Creator. Here, troubled hearts find solace; here, bewildered hearts find guidance. The power of the original Arabic is much stronger than any translation can convey. That is why it is advisable as one develops a relationship with the Qur'ān to begin to listen to and learn the Arabic. Sound resonates. This sound we can feel to the core of our being. For this reason, accompanying some

---

[5] Qur'ān: *Surah Taghābun*, 64:3
[6] Qur'ān: *Surah Qāf*, 50:7

of the key verses of the Qur'ān within these pages, I have included the Arabic transliteration, for those who might like to *take it to heart*.[7]

As it was said by 'Ali, a close companion of the Prophet Muhammad, and of the first of those to have faith in the message of the Qur'ān:

> Learn the Qur'ān, for it is the fairest of discourses, and understand it thoroughly, for it is the best blossoming of hearts. Seek remedy within its light, for it is the cure for hearts. And recite it beautifully, for it is the most beautiful narration.[8]

Within this Qur'ānic tradition, there is an immense beauty, an immense compassion, a sense of heart which could be of nourishment to many in the Western world who also find themselves thirsting in a "desert" even as Muhammad was thirsting before the coming of Revelation. Within Islam there is a stringency revealed—one must bear the consequences of one's actions; this is simply the law of nature, the law of karma, but as the Qur'ān, the Holy Book of Islam proclaims over and over again, at the commencement of each chapter or *surah*, *Bismillāhir Raḥmānir Raḥeem . . . In the Name of God, the Infinitely Compassionate and Most Merciful . . . .* This message is coming to us from the Compassionate womb of Creation. The root of the words *Raḥmān* and *Raḥeem* is the word for womb. Everything is held within the Compassion of our Source, and whatever stringency is manifested, it is always overwhelmed by and held within this Infinite Compassion.[9]

---

[7] Qur'ān: *Surah Ṣād*, 38:29.
[8] *Nahjul Balāghah* translated by Imām 'Ali 'ibn 'Abu Ṭālib: p.257.
[9] Qur'ān: *Surah 'Al-'A'rāf*, 7:56.

The Lord is Gracious; His Mercy is everlasting and His Truth endures forever. . . . These words from the Old Testament might be a verse from the Qur'ān, they are so similar in flavor and perspective. Many of the verses of the Qur'ān echo the beauty of the songs of David and Solomon, the clarity of the laws of Moses, the mystery and truth of the parables of Jesus. Unfortunately in the West, many Christians and Jews are unaware of this; few people are familiar with the beauty of the Qur'ān, the holy book of Islam. "Islam" means peace—the peace that comes with surrender, surrender to God. In the Qur'ān it is said that, *There is only one religion and it is surrender to God.*[10]

When all our actions are in consonance with the Divine Order and Will, we are surrendered to that Truth that is at the core of all that exists. The more it is possible for people of various spiritual traditions to recognize this unitive thread that ties us all together, the greater the possibility for peace—within ourselves and within this world in which we live.

In bringing forth this book of selected verses of the Qur'ān it is my wish to open a door so that people of any faith might recognize the Truth of the gracious mercy of God that manifests through the Qur'ān. It is a voice for wholeness, for unity, encouraging harmony within the human being and among human beings and their total environment. The truth conveyed through the Qur'ān is not different from the essential truth of Christianity or Judaism; it is not different from the essential message of Buddhism or Hinduism. The prophets all saw by the light of the same sun and spoke with the voice of the same Heart.

There need be no strife among us. God invites us to Unity— to *the abode of Peace.*[11] He invites us to *run the race for the good*[12] no

---

[10]Qur'ān: *Surah 'Āl 'Imrān*, 3:19.
[11]Qur'ān: *Surah Yūnis*, 10:25.
[12]Qur'ān: *Surah 'Al-Mā'idah*, 5:48

matter what our particular faith. In the Qur'ān it is recognized that we are diverse communities. God could have created us all as one—He could have *rooted the human being in one place*[13] that we might have no chance to stray. Instead, He gave us our freedom so that we might turn to Him with open heart, that we might know the joy of Love blossoming and coming to fruition and experience the whole range of feeling and knowing, discovering for ourselves the abundance of certainty. Within the Islamic tradition, it is expressed that even the angels were not strong enough to bear this challenge. Only the heart of the human being has the capacity to contain God; rather than a microcosm, the human being is the macrocosm. As Mevlana Jalaluddin Rumi says, "You are a dewdrop that contains the entire sea." What was revealed to the prophets and deeply understood by the wise might be revealed to our own hearts and minds if we would open to their words and truly listen.

And *God is the Light of the heavens and the earth*[14] and it is God *Who leads us out of the depths of darkness into the Light*[15] and Who has given the Qur'ān as *a clear light*[16] and *a mercy*[17] to all the worlds, to all levels of being.

Through the words of Mevlana Jalaluddin Rumi, many people have begun to be inclined towards exploring the Qur'ān. Through his references to the verses of the Qur'ān interwoven in his stories and poetry, the passages from the Qur'ān have begun to come alive for many who might otherwise never catch the light of its wisdom. Through Mevlana's eyes, we begin to see and hear a deeper meaning than at first acquaintance we might. As Mevlana says,

---

[13]Qur'ān: *Surah Yā Sīn*, 36:36.
[14]Qur'ān: *Surah An-Nur*, 24:35.
[15]Qur'ān: *Surah Al-Ahzab*, 33:42.
[16]Qur'ān: *Surah An-Nisa*, 4:174.
[17]Qur'ān: *Surah Al-'Ar'af*, 7:204.

When you read the Qur'ān
don't look only at the exterior, my son:
the Devil considers Adam as nothing more than clay.
The external sense of the Qur'ān is like a person's form:
while his features are visible, his spirit is hidden.
Someone's uncles look at him for a hundred years,
and yet of his inward state
don't see so much as the tip of a hair.
[*Mathnawi* III, 4247-4249][17]

As you read the verses included within this volume, I think you will recognize that the expanding universe of the Qur'ān is not foreign; it is the universe of Love within which we are already living, but perhaps have failed to see . . . . The Qur'ān calls to us to open our eyes and our hearts so we might witness that *Wherever you turn, there is the Face of God.*[18] For truly all around us *there are signs to see for those who reflect.*[19] May God guide us straight in our return to Him. May the Light of the words of the Qur'ān strengthen us in that which is right and enable us to live justly on this earth, without spreading corruption, and with tenderness and compassion towards each other, *lowering towards those who follow us the wings of tenderness.*[20] May the Light dawn within and all around us.

Camille Adams Helminski
'Eid ul 'Adha, 1997

---

[17] *Mathnawi* of Mevlana Jalaluddin Rumi: selected from *Jewels of Remembrance, a Daybook of Spiritual Guidance* translated by Camille and Kabir Helminski, Threshold Books, 1996.
[18] Qur'ān: *Surah Baqarah*, 2:11
[19] Qur'ān: *Surah 'Al-Jāthiyah*, 45:13.
[20] Qur'ān: *Surah 'Ash-Shu'arā'*

A Note on Translation

It is my hope that the verses rendered here may bring light to your heart. May God forgive me for whatever mistakes may have occurred in this humble attempt . . . I owe an inestimable debt of gratitude to those who have previously completed translations of the Qur'ān into English whose work has brought me great sustenance and who have been my mentors in the process of rendering these selections, especially Muhammad Asad and Yusuf Ali. It is with the help of their translations and that of others, as well as the original Arabic, that I have sought to render some of the verses of the Qur'ān that I have found to be of greatest nourishment. In any one moment though, the Light of any of its verses may become manifest to a heart that is open to receive that Light. For God guides to His light the one who wills to be guided.[21] And for those who respond to His guidance, He increases His guidance.[22] I pray that this small volume may be of help in this process.

Regarding the use of pronouns . . . in some cases I have used the feminine pronoun rather than the masculine for both the human being and occasionally in reference to God so that those reading these selections may have a reminder that within the Universe and understanding of the Qur'ān, God is without gender, *Truly, Our Sustainer is beyond anything by which we may seek to define Him/Her.*[23] The Qur'ān is one of the few Holy Books with which I am familiar which speaks directly to both "men who have faith" and "women who have faith" in numerous passages. In God's sight, men and women are equal; what matters is not gender, wealth, or power, but that we bring to our Sustainer *a sound heart*[24] when we return to Our Source. It is these who shall find themselves abiding in the

---

[21] Qur'ān: *Surah 'An-Nūr*, 24:35.
[22] Qur'ān: *Surah Muḥammad*, 47:17
[23] Qur'ān: *Surah 'Aṣ-Ṣāffāt*, 37:180
[24] Qur'ān: *Surah Ash-Shu'arā'*, 26:89

Garden, now and eternally . . . a Garden underneath which rivers flow, and where everywhere one is met with the greeting, "*Peace*."[25]

O God! Grant me Light in my heart,
Light in my grave,
Light in front of me, Light behind me,
Light to my right, Light to my left,
Light above me, Light below me,
Light in my ears, Light in my eyes,
Light in my skin, Light in my hair,
Light within my flesh, Light in my blood, Light in my bones.
O God! Increase my Light everywhere.
O God! Grant me Light in my heart, Light on my tongue,
Light in my eyes, Light in my ears,
Light to my right, Light to my left,
Light above me, Light below me,
Light in front of me, Light behind me,
and Light within my self; increase my Light.

~ Muhammad's Prayer of Light

[25] Qur'ān: *Surah Yā sīn*, 36:58

Acknowledgements

All thanks be to God,
the Infinitely Compassionate and Most Merciful.

Many thanks are due to Dr. Refik Algan,
for his inspiration, his continuously generous support, and friendship;
to Dr. Asad Ali, for his example—
his delight in and ability to be instructed
and inspired by this Living Word;
to my beloved husband, Kabir, and our beloved children,
Matthew, Shams, and Cara,
for the Light of their being and their patience;
to Michael Wolfe for his helpful suggestions
and brotherly support of this project;
to Imam Bilal Hyde and Imam Feisal Rauf
for their friendship and encouragement of this work;
to Mahmoud Mostafa
for his careful consideration of and assistance
with the appropriate manner of transliteration;
and to all the friends of Threshold
whose yearning
has helped to bring this project to fruition.

Transliteration Key

Prepared by Mahmoud Mostafa

Arabic letter	Symbol	Sound	Arabic letter	Symbol	Sound
1. hamzah	ʾ	a	15. ḍāḍ	ḍ	double
2. beh	b	bee	16. ṭah	ṭ	trout
3. teh	t	tea	17. ẓah	ẓ	thou
4. theh	th	theme	18. ʿayn	ʿ	gutteral a
5. jīm	j	gem	19. ghain	gh	gutteral g
6. ḥah	ḥ	gutteral h	20. feh	f	father
7. khah	kh	gutteral k	21. qāf	q	acquire
8. dāl	d	date	22. kāf	k	keen
9. zhāl	zh	the	23. lām	l	lean
10. reh	r	ray	24. mīm	m	moon
11. zain	z	zoo	25. nūn	n	noon
12. sīn	s	see	26. heh	h	heal
13. shīn	sh	show	27. waw	w	with
14. ṣāḍ	ṣ	such	28. yeh	y	you
Vowels					
Short Vowels			**Long Vowels**		
1. Fat-ḥa	a	at	29. Aah	ā	far
2. Kasrah	i	in	30. Uuh	ū	moon
3. Ḍammah	u	put	31. Eeh	ī	sheet
Elongated Vowels					
Used when reciting at the end of a verse *or in the middle when a vowel is followed by a hamzah*					
Elongated Aah	aa	Elongated Uuh	uu	Elongated Eeh	ee

Introduction
The Living Word

Once I asked a certain shaikh if he had any advice about how to read the Qurʾān, the sacred text of Islam. His answer has remained imprinted in my mind and heart: "When you read it as if you were reading the word of God, it will open its secrets to you."

What could it mean to call a spiritual text the word of God? Long ago I stopped believing in such absolutes. If ever I had "blind faith," it was shattered by my early teens when I began to read the existentialists—Neitzsche, Camus, Heidigger. By my college years I was at home with Lao Tzu, Padma Sambhava, and Hui Neng. Only much later did I finally meet the masters of Islamic spirituality: 'Attar, Ibn 'Arabi, and Jalaluddin Rumi. None of the writings of these masters, though supremely inspired, could have been described as "the word of God."

And, in fact, these Sufi writings were sometimes presented as teachings for initiates that transcended the exoteric religious teaching presented by prophets for the masses. The assumption was that mystics of a certain attainment showed respect to the outer religion of their society but became universal beings inwardly free of all forms. In certain spiritual circles the great Sufis were selectively quoted with an emphasis on their most unitive states in which they uttered truths that seemed to support the formless, eclectic "truth" that many people in the West had arrived at after some meditation, or other altered states of consciousness.

Didn't Rumi, for instance, say: "What shall I do, O Muslims, for I do not recognize myself? I am neither Christian, nor Jew, nor Magian, nor Muslim." And the great Turkish bard, Yunus Emre, could say: "Truth is an ocean; the Sacred Law is a ship. But the sea can always smash the ship and many have never plunged into the Ocean."

What was not obvious was that the classical Sufis presupposed a certain acceptance of the stabilizing principles of Islamic practice and the revelation of the Qur'ān. Their radical and ecstatic utterances were intended within their own context to urge people beyond an identification with unexamined assumptions and forms. Nevertheless, they themselves considered the "way of Muhammad," *as they understood it,* to be their own true path, and the Qur'ānic revelation as the one pure, inexhaustible spring of wisdom and guidance.

In fact it is in these writers that we meet the Qur'ān in its most accessible form. We find them continually quoting from or alluding to the Qur'ān, and we begin to have a sense of the depths of meaning to be found in this Book. Some Sufi shaikhs even recommend that students first approach the Qur'ān through the writings of the "friends of God," the *awliya,* before one approaches the Qur'ān directly. I suspect two reasons for this. Mevlana Rumi said, "The Qur'ān is a shy bride." It is better to meet her through a close friend. Equally true, the Qur'ān is a mirror and what we will see in this mirror will be a reflection of ourselves and this reflection may include our own shadow.

It is not uncommon for first-time Western readers to see the Divine wrath in this mirror, and there is no doubt that the Qur'ān is full of warning. It tirelessly warns of the dire consequences for those who transgress "against their own souls," and "spread corruption upon the earth." The Qur'ān is a book that comprehends the whole of human life, and if we look at the history of human life on this earth, we must admit the terrible consequences of human selfishness and cruelty.

Revelation, being the complete and unsentimentalized Truth, must delineate both the mercy and the wrath. And yet in the Qur'ān it is said, "My Mercy is greater than My Wrath." In fact, from the highest point of view there is even more "mercy" in the *wrath* than there is wrath. The stringency of the wrath is simply the lawful consequence of turning our backs to Reality. And yet this "stringency" is also "mercy" in so far as it may turn us in the direction of Truth, may reconnect us with our Source.

The Qur'ān is important to us today for many reasons. To begin with, it is one of the two most influential books in human history. Like the Bible it has been read, memorized, and accepted as a guide to everyday life by billions of people. Moreover, the Qur'ān is considered the foremost miracle of Islam.

Fourteen centuries ago the Qur'ān and the Prophet who received it so magnetized a backward and feuding people that their spiritual conviction spread through most of the known world in little more than a century. For the next thousand years the principles derived from the Qur'ān and the example of Muhammad created a relatively unified and just society, characterized by a high level of personal sanctity, generosity of spirit, and social justice. It was a world culture in which religious pluralism was accepted, women obtained more rights than in most other societies, class exploitation was lessened, science flourished side by side with religion, and mysticism permeated everyday life. Contrary to popular conceptions, it was a society relatively free of interpersonal and sectarian violence. One only has to compare it with the relatively abysmal conditions in most of the world to see that something extraordinary had been established. The influence of the Qur'ān set in motion a spiritual and social transformation of a magnitude that has not been surpassed by any ideology in the history of human life. Regrettably, the last few centuries have seen a gradual degeneration and stagnation within most Islamic societies, which was further accelerated by negative impacts both during and following the colonialist period. Yet even this unpropitious period does not belie the power of the Book that shaped a civilization.

The Qur'ān is a book of spiritual guidance that offers a knowledge of the structure of reality and the purpose of human life. It challenges the human being to become fully human and conscious of God. The level of personal work that it asks of the average human being is very high. It outlines a way of life and spiritual practice that would put Divine Reality into the center of human consciousness.

This book also deserves the careful attention of anyone drawn to the words of the great classical Sufi authors. Every major Sufi master from Bistami to Hallaj, from Ibn 'Arabi to Shamsi Tabriz and Rumi, from Hazrat Inayat Khan to Bawa Muhaiyadeen, has acknowledged the centrality and authenticity of the Qur'ān.

The influence of the Qur'ān has been a major uplifting agency in human affairs. It asks us to become people:

whom neither business nor possessions can divert from the remembrance of God, nor from constancy in prayer, nor from the practice of regular charity, and who remain ever vigilant regarding that day when hearts and eyes will be transformed. [24:37]

The Qur'ān should be approached and judged on its own terms.

It is God who sent down to you in truth the Book, confirming what went before it, Who sent down the Law (of Moses) and the Gospel before this as a guide to humankind, and Who (now) has revealed the Criterion. [3:3]

Will they not, then, try to understand this Qur'ān? Had it issued from any but God, they would surely have found in it many inner contradictions. [4:82]

And if you doubt any part of what We have bestowed from on high, step by step, upon Our servant, then produce a surah of similar merit, and call upon any other than God to bear witness for you—if what you say is true. [2:23]

As the selections above suggest, the Qur'ān is a book without internal contradictions. It is from the same source as previous revelations, including those of Moses and Jesus. Finally, for those who can hear it and understand it in Arabic, the tongue of its revelation, the Qur'ān is expressed in a language of unsurpassed depth and beauty.

To begin to appreciate what the Qur'ān is, it is necessary to understand the unique circumstances of its revelation. Virtually every other religious canon can be shown to be the product of various human minds telling a story, or commenting upon the experience of an enlightened being. We have such texts within Islam as well. A few may contain the words of the prophet or the enlightened being themselves, although most of these are likely to be spuriously mixed with words of known or unknown attribution, as in the case of the Gospels, for instance. The *hadith,* or sayings of Muhammad, having been subjected to the most rigorous historical criteria, nevertheless cannot be proven to be wholly free of fabrication or distortion. The Qur'ān itself is in a unique position both in terms of how it was preserved, and even more importantly how it was received.

Muhammad at age forty was a respected member of the Quraysh tribe of Mecca and a manager of caravans financed by his wife Khadija. He was an independent seeker in a commercial, tribal society that placed very little value on spirituality. From time to time he would seclude himself in a cave on Mount Hira for the purpose of spiritual retreat. One night in the cave a handsome being appeared, who said to him, "Recite."

"But I cannot, " Muhammad replied.

Again the being commanded him, and again Muhammad declined. Finally, the being took him in a crushing embrace, released him, and said, "Recite, in the name of your Lord, who created humankind from a germ cell . . . "

Muhammad was terrified by the experience and rushed home to his wife. "Cover me," he pleaded, "for I may be losing my mind." Khadija reassured him that a man such as he was very unlikely to lose his mind. She consulted with her uncle, Waraqa, a wise man with an inclination toward Christian belief. Waraqa, upon hearing the exact words given by the strange being in the cave, believed that Muhammad had been visited by the Archangel Gabriel and had received a revelation such as had been received by the prophets of earlier times.

This first revelation to Muhammad was followed by a silence of many months, and then the revelations began to be more regular. The effect on Muhammad was overwhelming—he would sweat, he would cover himself; sometimes the revelations arrived while he was riding a camel and the camel would fall to its knees unable to hold him in that state.

The chapters of the revelation frequently came to Muhammad in response to the circumstances of his life. It was as if a dialogue had begun between one man and the Intelligence of the universes. It was a dialogue both specifically addressed to Muhammad and yet of universal application. It came in a language of such inimitable beauty and power that people frequently wept upon hearing it.

The Qurʾān is a revelation communicated in the clear light of historical time. It came through Muhammad but was clearly not from Muhammad. He was, after all, a man who, despite his widely recognized sincerity and trustworthiness, was unlettered and had very little exposure to or knowledge of the religious traditions of the world. Nevertheless, the Qurʾān has a quality of its own, of a different literary order than the sayings of the Prophet himself (which have been preserved and which also form an important part of the Islamic tradition). The Qurʾān is a call to recognize the order and beneficence of the seen and unseen worlds, promising happiness and peace for those whose hearts can hear, and unhappiness and ruin for those who spread corruption. It is a plea to human beings to recognize the good and to cease destroying their own souls.

The Qurʾān is said to have been transmitted from Allah by the Archangel Gabriel, who is understood to be the archetypal intelligence of humanity. Human language strains and is almost torn apart by the power of this revelation. The first-time reader is confronted with a text as avant garde, in a sense, as any modern writing produced in this century. Its non-linearity leads one into a timeless universe; its multiplicity of ideas, images, and symbols all point and refer to a master Truth of Divine Beneficence. It offers to the restless human mind a vast landscape of detail and meaning that gradually leads to the realization of the unity of Being. It shifts our concerns from multiplicity to one underlying Compassionate Reality.

The Word

The Word (*al-Kalimah*) can be understood as that which establishes and confirms the relationship between the Divine and the human. What the Divine speaks to humanity concerns Reality and Truth (*al-Haqq*) [6:73]. It is given to human beings as a clear guidance amid the tests of this earthly life. The Revelation is meant to be reflected upon, taken into ourselves and then: *His Word will find its fulfillment in sincerity and justice.* [6:115]

> *Aren't you aware how God sets forth the likeness of a good word? It is firmly rooted like a good tree, its branches reaching toward the sky, yielding its fruit at all times by the permission of its Sustainer.*
>
> *And in this way God sets forth likenesses for human beings, so that they might reflect upon the truth.*
>
> *And the likeness of a corrupt word is that of a corrupt tree, torn up upon the face of the earth, unable to endure.*
>
> *God grants firmness to those who have attained faith through the word that is unshakably true in the life of this world as well as in the life to come; but the wrongdoers are allowed to stray, and God does as He wills.* [14:24-27]

The Word will also stand against those who deny what is Real, the lawful order, and, as the Qur²ān often reminds, will be a proof against them. Muhammad Asad suggests that "the word" often means "promise," that "the word" is the promise of the Divine to humanity.

In its wider meaning, the term *kalimah* ("word") denotes any conceptual statement or proposition. Thus a "good word" circumscribes any proposition (or idea) that is intrinsically true and—because it implies a call to what is good in the oral sense—is ultimately beneficent and enduring; and since a call to moral righteousness is the innermost purport of every one of God's messages, the term "good word" applies to them as well. Similarly, "the corrupt word" mentioned in verse 26 applies to the opposite of what the divine message aims at: namely, to every idea that is intrinsically false or morally evil and, therefore, spiritually harmful.[26]

Although it is unlikely that Muhammad had any direct contact with the New Testament, "The Word of God" as presented in the Qur²ān is remarkably consistent with the notion of the "word" as expressed in the New Testament: "Man does not live by bread alone, but by every word that proceeds from the mouth of God." Furthermore, in the Qur²ān Jesus, himself, is referred to as a "word" from God.

According to Seyyed Hossein Nasr:

The Word of God in Islam is the Quran; in Christianity it is Christ. The vehicle of the Divine Message in Christianity is the Virgin Mary; in Islam it is the soul of the Prophet. The Prophet must be unlettered

---

[26] *Message of the Qur'an*, Muhammad Asad, p.36

for the same reason that the Virgin Mary must be virgin. The human vehicle of a Divine Message must be pure and untainted. The Divine Word can only be written on the pure and 'untouched' tablet of human receptivity. If this Word is in the form of flesh the purity is symbolized by the virginity of the mother who gives birth to the Word, and if it is in the form of a book this purity is symbolized by the unlettered nature of the person who is chosen to announce the Word among men. . . . The unlettered nature of the Prophet demonstrates how the human recipient is completely passive before the Divine. Were this purity and virginity of the soul not to exist, the Divine Word would in a sense become tainted with purely human knowledge and not be presented to mankind in its pristine purity.[27]

The Qurʾān refers to itself as *guidance for humanity* [2:185]. Its task is to awaken faith in and awareness of the Unseen Beneficence. Allah, the only God of all religions, is the Master Truth of existence. The Qurʾān speaks often and in many contexts about God, and all of these contexts must be interiorized into a wholeness in order to do justice to the Qurʾān's message. The Qurʾān works by drawing our attention to certain evident facts—primarily the beauty, order, and intelligence evidenced in human nature and the natural world—and turning these facts into "reminders" of the existence of a benevolent Unseen Intelligence.

The Qurʾān has the ability to speak directly to the majority of human beings through concrete images and to address their daily needs with an essentially uncomplicated message. Beyond its apparent simplicity, however, it has served as a source of inspiration to the deepest souls and held the interest of the greatest intellects of

---

[27] *Ideals and Realities of Islam*, Seyyid Hossein Nasr, p.43

every age. This ability to touch the minds and hearts of all kinds of human beings is one sign of its Divine origin.

The verses of the Qur'ān are not called verses but *"ayats,"* literally signs. The same word is used in describing the perceptions that are offered to the person of faith.

> *In time We shall make them fully understand Our signs in the farthest horizons and within themselves, so that it will become clear to them that this [revelation] is indeed the truth. Is it not enough to know that your Sustainer is a witness to everything?* [41:53]

The apprehension of these signs depends not only upon our faculty of reason, but also upon the cognitive powers of the heart. The Qur'ān mentions the kind of human being

> . . . *Who is humble before the Unseen and brings a heart that can respond.* [50:33]

It says further that:

> *It is a reminder to whomever has a heart and surrenders his/her ears to witnessing.* [50:37]

Approaching the Qur'ān

Reading the Qur'ān in translation is not really reading the Qur'ān at all, but a mere paraphrase of its meanings. This problem is compounded by the tendency of Qur'ānic translations to take their cues from the theologized conventions of Biblical translation. These conventions are arguably insufficient to translate even the Gospels because they transpose the simple and direct Greek of the New Testament into a theological language that developed centuries later. To try to make the Qur'ān sound like a translation of the Bible is to dress it in missionary clothes.

Even some of the best translations are subject to striking distortions of this type, as for example, these lines from Yusuf Ali's translation: *"Our religion is the baptism of Allah: And who can baptize better than Allah? And it is He Whom we worship."* [II, 138] Compare this with Muhammad Asad's translation: *"Say: 'Our life takes its hue from God! And who could give a better hue to life than God, if we but truly worship Him?'"*

The idea of a sacred language is relatively foreign and unfamiliar to the modern secular world. The text of the New Testament, for instance, would not generally be thought to have more efficacy in its original Greek than in a modern vernacular language. The language in which Jesus himself delivered his message, Aramaic, has practically disappeared from the face of the earth. The Roman Catholic Church used Latin as a sacred language for centuries, but now that has been eroded. Likewise the sacred texts of Buddhism may be in Sanskrit, Chinese, Tibetan, or Japanese. These faiths depend instead on a sacred individual, as the primary spiritual manifestation, namely Jesus or Buddha, more than they do on a sacred text and language.

Hinduism, Judaism, and Islam, on the other hand, are faiths based on sacred books and sacred language in which a Divine Presence operates through language itself. In Islam there is a grace, a *baraka*, that is embodied in the language of the Qur'ān. To recite or write the Qur'ān is a sacred act. The Divine text gradually becomes the universe in which one lives, its language being a living environment, its words providing a spiritual nourishment.

The essence of revelation is to remind us of our origin and nature after we have forgotten. It is the remedy for our ontological amnesia. All of God's qualities have been kneaded into the bread of the human being with the pure water of God's love. The water that made the bread possible has been forgotten. Mevlana Jalaluddin Rumi said:

God has sent prophets and saints, like great clear waters, in order that the dark and murky waters touched by the clear waters might free themselves of their coincidental murkiness and discoloration. The murky water then "remembers." When it sees itself clear, it realizes that it was originally clear and that its murkiness and discoloration are coincidental. It recalls how it was before the advent of these coincidentals and says, *"This is what we were formerly sustained by"* [2:25]. Prophets and saints, therefore, are "reminders" of one's past condition. They do not put anything new into one's substance. Now every murky water that recognizes that Great Water and says, "I am from and of this," mingles with It. But murky waters, that do not recognize that Water and think they are different or of another type, withdraw so into their murkiness and discoloration that they are unable to mingle with the Sea. They become ever more estranged from the Sea.[28]

To approach the Qurʾān requires that we prepare ourselves to be receptive to it. It requires that we get in touch with the deeper dimensions of our own being. Mevlana Jalaluddin Rumi in his *Fihi ma Fihi* has this to say about approaching the Qurʾān:

The Qurʾān is like a shy bride. Although you pull aside her veil, she will not show you her face. The reason you have no pleasure or discovery in all your study of it is that it rejects your attempt to pull off its veil. It tricks you and shows itself to you as ugly, as if to say, "I am not that beauty." It is capable of showing any face it wants. If, on the other hand, you do not tug at the veil, but you acquiesce, give water to its sown field, do it service from afar and try to do what pleases it without pulling at its

---

[28] *Fihi ma Fihi*, Mevlana Jalaluddin Rumi, Discourse Eight.

veil, it will show you its face. Seek the people of God, *enter among my servants; and enter my paradise* [89:29-30].

God does not speak to just anyone, as kings in this world do not speak to every weaver. They appoint viziers and deputies through whom people can reach them. So also has God selected a certain servant to the end that whoever seeks God can find Him through that servant. All the prophets have come for the sole reason that they are the way.[29]

If the Qur'ān can contribute to our discovering within ourselves that same Source that first revealed this book to Muhammad, then it will have accomplished the essential work of all spirituality—to reconnect the isolated human being with the Intelligence and Love of the universes, the Source of all that is.

~ Kabir Helminski
Putney, Vermont

---

[29] *Fihi ma Fihi,* Mevlana Jalaluddin Rumi, Discourse Sixty-Five.

The Light *of* Dawn

Daily Readings from the Holy Qur'ān

The Opening

Al-Fātiḥa

In the Name of God, the Infinitely Compassionate, Most Merciful.
All praise is God's,
the Sustainer of all worlds,
the Infinitely Compassionate and Most Merciful,
Sovereign of the Day of Reckoning.
You alone do we worship,
and You alone do we ask for help.
Guide us on the straight path—
the path of those who have received Your favor,
not the path of those who have earned Your wrath,
nor of those who have gone astray.

Bismillāhir Raḥmānir Raḥeem.
ʾAlḥamdu lillāhi rabbil ʿālameen.
ʾArraḥmānir Raḥeem.
Māliki yawmid deen.
ʾIyyāka naʿbudu wa ʾiyyāka nastaʿeen.
ʾIhdināṣ ṣirāṭal mustaqeem.
Ṣirāṭal lazhīna ʾanʿamta ʿalayhim
ghayril maghḍūbi ʿalayhim wa laḍ ḍaalleen.

[1:1-7]

The Cow

Al-Baqarah

O Humankind!
Worship your Sustainer, who has created you
and those who lived before you,
so that you might remain conscious of the One
who has made the earth a resting-place for you and the sky a canopy,
and has sent water down from the sky
and with it brought forth fruits for your sustenance:
then don't claim that there is any power that could rival God,
when you grasp the truth.

[2:21-22]

Truly: all who surrender their whole being to God,
and do good, shall have their reward with their Sustainer;
these need have no fear, neither shall they grieve.

[2:112]

To God belong the east and the west.
Wherever you turn, there is the face of God.
Witness, God is infinite, all-knowing.

Wa lillāhil mashriqu wal maghrib.
Fa-ʾaynamā tuwallu fathamma wajhullāhi.
ʾInnallāha wāsiʿun ʿaleem.

[2:115]

O you who have attained to faith!
Seek help through steadfast patience and prayer:
for observe, God is with those who patiently persevere.

[2:153]

Look around you!—
In the creation of the heavens and the earth;
in the alternation of night and day;
in the sailing of ships through the ocean for the profit of humankind;
in the waters which God sends down from the skies
and the life which the One gives by means of it to an earth that is dead;
in the living creatures of all kinds which multiply there;
in the change of the winds
and the clouds that follow, between sky and earth;
truly, these are signs for people who reflect.

[2:164]

3

O you who have attained to faith! Fasting is ordained for you
as it was ordained for those before you,
so that you might remain conscious of God.

[2:183]

And whoever does more good than he/she is bound to do
thereby does good to himself/herself;
for to fast is to do good to yourselves—if you only knew it.

[2:184]

And if My servants ask you about Me—witness, I am near;
I respond to the call of the one who calls,
whenever he calls Me:
let them, then, respond to Me, and have faith in Me,
so that they may follow the right way.

*Wa ʾizha saʾalaka ʿibādī ʿannī faʾinnī qareebun
ʾujību daʿwatad dāʿi ʾizhā daʿaani
falyastajībū lī walyuʾminū bī laʿallahum yarshuduun.*

[2:186]

Be continuously mindful of prayers,
and of praying in the most excellent way;
and stand before God in devoted surrender.

[2:238]

God—there is no deity but Hu,[30]
the Ever-Living, the Self-Subsisting Source of all Being.
No slumber can seize Him/Her nor sleep.
All things in heaven and on earth belong to Hu.
Who could intercede in His/Her Presence
without His/Her permission?
He/She knows what appears in front of and behind His/Her creatures.
Nor can they encompass any knowledge of Him/Her
except what He/She wills.
His/Her throne extends over the heavens and the earth,
and He/She feels no fatigue in guarding and preserving them,
for He/She is the Highest and Most Exalted.

ʾAllāhu laa ʾilāha ʾillā huwal ḥayyul qayyuum.
Lā taʾkhuzhuhu sinatun wa lā nawm.
Lahu mā fis samāwati wa mā fil arḍ.
Manzhal lazhī yashfaʿu ʿindahu ʾillā biʾizhnih.
Yaʿlamu mā bayna ʾaydīhim wa mā khalfahum
wa lā yuḥīṭuna bishayʾim min ʿilmihee ʾillā bimā shaaʾ.
Wasiʿa kursiyyuhus samāwati wal ʾarḍa wa lā yaʾūduhu
ḥifẓuhumā. Wa huwal ʿaliyyul ʿaẓeem.

[2:255]

30*Hu*: the pronoun of Divine Presence. All words in Arabic have a gender grammatically ascribed to them as they do in French and Spanish, etc. Although *Allah* is referred to with the third person masculine pronoun *Hu* (*Huwa*), it is universally understood that *Allah's* Essence is beyond gender or indeed any qualification. In this translation occasionally *Hu* will be used and sometimes "He/She" in an attempt to avoid the mistake of attributing human gender to That which is beyond all our attempts at definition, limitless in subtle glory.

Let there be no compulsion in matters of faith.

[2:256]

God is the Protector of those who have faith,
leading them out of the depths of darkness into the light.

'Allāhu waliyyul lazhīna 'āmanu
yukhrijuhum minaz zulūmāti 'ilannuur.

[2:257]

O you who have faith!
Spend on others out of the good things which you may have acquired,
and out of that which We[31] bring forth for you out of the earth;
and do not choose for your spending
anything bad which you yourselves would not accept
without averting your eyes in disdain.
And know that God is the One Who is Rich,
the One Worthy of Praise.
Satan threatens you with the prospect of poverty
and bids you to be stingy,
while God promises you His forgiveness and abundance;
and God is infinite, all knowing,
granting wisdom to whom He wills:
and whoever is granted wisdom
has indeed been granted abundant wealth,
but none bears this in mind
except those who are gifted with insight.

[2:267-9]

---

[31]In the revelation of the Qur'ān, the Divine Source sometimes chooses to speak
or refer to Itself from the first person singular, *I/Me*, sometimes as the third
person singular, and sometimes as the first person plural, *We*. Some commentators
suggest that the usage of *We* refers to the attributes of God.

The messenger, and the faithful with him,
have faith in what has been revealed to him by his Sustainer:
they all have faith in God, and His angels,
and His revelations, and His messengers,
making no distinction between any of His messengers;
and they say: "We have heard, and we pay heed.
Grant us Your forgiveness, O our Sustainer,
for with You is all journeys' end!"
God does not burden any human being
with more than he can bear:
in his favor shall be whatever good he does,
and against him whatever harm he does.

"O our Sustainer!
Do not take us to task if we forget or unknowingly do wrong!
O our Sustainer! Do not lay upon us a burden
like that which You placed on those who lived before us!
O our Sustainer! Do not make us bear burdens
which we have no strength to bear!
And efface our sins, and grant us forgiveness,
and bestow Your mercy on us!
You are our Supreme Lord: help us when we face those who stand
against truth."

[2:285–6]

The House of Imran

ʾĀl ʿImrān

God—there is no god but Hu,[32]
the Ever-Living, the Self-Subsisting Source of all Being.

ʾAllāhu laa ʾilāha ʾillā huwal ḥayyul qayyuum.

[3:2]

Step by step He has sent down to you this book,
setting forth the truth which confirms
whatever remains of earlier revelations:
for it is He who earlier bestowed from on high
the Torah and the Gospel, as a guidance to humankind,
and it is He who has bestowed the standard for discernment.
Witness:
grievous suffering awaits
those who are bent on denying God's signs—
for God is Almighty, the Avenger of Evil.
Truly, nothing on earth or in the heavens is hidden from God.
It is He who shapes you in the wombs as He wills.
There is no deity but Hu, the Almighty, the Truly Wise.

[3:3-6]

---

[32] See previous note 30.

8

"O our Sustainer!
Do not let our hearts swerve from the truth
after You have guided us;
and bestow on us the gift of Your grace:
truly, You are the Giver of Gifts."

Rabbanā lā tuzigh qulūbanā
baʿda ʾizh hadaytanā
wa hab lanā milladunka raḥmatan
ʾinnaka ʾantal wahhāb.

[3:8]

Witness, the only true religion in the sight of God
is self-surrender to Him.

[3:19]

Whenever Zachariah visited her in the sanctuary,
he found her provided with food. He would ask,
"O Mary, from where did this come to you?"
She would answer: "It is from God;
see how God grants sustenance to whom He wills,
beyond all reckoning."

[3:37]

Never shall you attain righteousness unless you spend on others
out of what you yourselves truly love;
and whatever you spend—certainly, God knows.

[3:92]

O you who have faith!
Be conscious of God with all the consciousness that is due Him,
and do not allow death to overtake you
before you have surrendered yourselves to Him.
And hold fast, all together, to the rope of God,
and do not draw apart from one another.
And remember with gratitude the blessings
which God has bestowed on you:
how, when you were adversaries, He brought your hearts together,
so that through His blessings you became as though of one family;
and how when you were on the brink of a fiery abyss,
He saved you from it.
In this way, God makes clear His signs to you,
so that you might be guided,
and that there might grow out of you a community
who invite to all that is good, and encourage the doing of what is right
and forbid the doing of what is wrong:
and it is they who shall attain happiness!

[3:102-4]

To God belongs all that is in the heavens
and all that is on earth;
and all things are returning to God.

*Wa lillāhi mā fissamāwāti
wa mā fil ʾarḍ.
Wa ʾilallāhi turjaʿul ʾumuur.*

[3:109]

Strive among yourselves to attain your Sustainer's forgiveness
and a paradise as vast as the heavens and the earth,
which has been readied for those who are conscious of God—
who spend in His way in times of abundance and in times of hardship,
and hold in check their anger,
and pardon their fellow human beings,
because God loves those who do good;
and who, when they have committed a shameful deed
or have otherwise wronged their own souls,
remember God
and pray for forgiveness for their mistakes—
for who can forgive sins but God?—
and do not knowingly persist
in doing whatever wrong they may have done.

[3:133-5]

Many ways of life have passed away before your time.
Go, then, about the earth and see what happened
in the end to those who denied the truth:
here is a clear lesson for all human beings
and a guidance and a counsel for those who are conscious of God.
So do not lose heart, nor fall into despair:
for if you are faithful you are bound to ascend.

[3:137-9]

You shall most certainly be tried in your possessions and in yourselves;
and indeed you shall hear much that will cause you grief
from those to whom revelation was granted before your time,
as well as from those
who have come to attribute divinity to others beside God.
But if you persevere and remain conscious of Hu[33]—
see how this is something on which to set one's heart.

[3:186]

---

[33] See previous note 30.

And to God belongs the dominion over the heavens and the earth;
and God has power over all things.
Truly, in the creation of the heavens and the earth,
and in the succession of night and day,
there are indeed signs for all who are endowed with insight,
and who remember God standing, and sitting,
and when they lie down to sleep,
and contemplate creation—of the heavens and the earth:
"O our Sustainer!
You have not created this without meaning and purpose.
Limitless are You in Your subtle glory!"

[3:189-91]

O you who have come to faith!
Be patient, and persevere in patience,
and keep your connection,
and remain conscious of God,
so that you might attain felicity.

Yaa ʾayyuhal lazhīna ʾāmanuṣbiru
wa ṣābiru wa rābiṭu
wattaqullāha laʿallakum tuflihuun.

[3:200]

Women

'An-Nisā'

Truly, God does not wrong anyone by as much as an atom's weight;
and if there is a good deed, He will compound it
and will bestow out of His Presence a mighty recompense.

*'Innallāha lā yaẓlimu mithqāla zharratin
wa 'intaku ḥasanatan yuḍā'ifehā
wa yu'tī milladunhu 'ajeran 'aẓīmaa*

[4:40]

Witness, God instructs you
to deliver all that you have been entrusted with
to those who are entitled to it,
and whenever you judge between people, to judge with justice.
Truly, how excellent is that which God urges you to do;
truly, God is All-hearing, All-seeing.

[4:58]

For all those who listen to God and the Messenger
are among those on whom God has bestowed His blessings:
the prophets, and those who never deviated from the truth,
and those who with their lives bore witness to the truth,
and the righteous ones; and what a beautiful friendship this is.
Such is the abundance of God—
and it suffices that God is All-Knowing.

Wa man yuṭiʿ illāha war-rasula
faʾulaaʾika maʿallazhīna ʾanʿamallāhu
ʿalayhim minan nabiyyīna waṣṣidiqīna
wash-shuhadaaʾi waṣṣāliḥīn.
Wa ḥasuna ʾulaaʾika rafīqaa.
Zhālikal faḍlu minallāh.
Wa kafā billāhi ʿalīmaa.

[4:69-70]

Whoever supports a good cause shall have a share in its blessings;
and whoever supports an evil cause shall be answerable for his part in it:
for, indeed, God watches over everything.
But when you are greeted with a greeting of peace,
answer with an even better greeting, or at least with its like.
Truly, God keeps count of all things.
God—there is no god but Hu[34]—
will surely gather you all together
on the Day when the Everlasting stands,
the coming of which is beyond all doubt;
and whose word could be truer than God's?

[4:85-87]

---

[34] See previous note 30.

15

O you who have faith! When you go forth in God's cause
use your discernment and do not—
out of a desire for the fleeting gains of this worldly life—
say to anyone who offers you a greeting: "You are not of the faithful!"
for with God are abundant benefits.
You, too, were once in the same condition—
but God has been gracious to you:
so use your discernment: truly, God is well-aware of all that you do.

[4:94]

When you have finished your prayer, remember God—
standing, and sitting, and lying down;
and when you are once again secure, observe your prayers.
Truly, for all the faithful prayer is a sacred duty
joined to particular times.

[4:103]

Anyone—be it man or woman—who does good deeds
and is of the faithful, shall enter the Garden,
and shall not be wronged by as much as the groove on the pit of a date.
And who could be of better faith
than the one who surrenders his or her whole being to God
and is a doer of good,
and follows the Way of Abraham, the true in faith—
seeing that God chose Abraham for a beloved friend?
For, to God belongs all that is in the heavens and on earth;
and indeed God encompasses all things.

[4:124-126]

If one desires the rewards of this world,
let him remember that with God are the rewards
of both this world and the life to come;
and God is indeed All-Hearing, All-Seeing.

[4:134]

O you who have attained to faith!
Always be steadfast in upholding justice,
bearing witness to the truth for God's sake,
even though it may be against your own selves
or your parents and kinsfolk.
Whether the person concerned be rich or poor,
God's claim takes precedence over the claims of either.
Do not, then, follow your own desires,
that you might not turn aside from that which is just.
For if you distort the truth, witness,
God is indeed well-aware of all that you do!

[4:135]

As for those who have faith in God and His messengers
and make no distinctions between any of them—
to them, in time, will He grant their recompense.
And God is indeed Ever Ready to Forgive, Most Merciful.

[4:152]

Never did the Messiah feel too proud to be God's servant,
nor do the angels who are near to Him.
And those who feel too proud to serve Him
and glory in their arrogance should know
that He will gather them all to Himself.

[4:172]

O humankind!
A manifestation of the truth has now come to you
from your Sustainer,
and We have sent to you a clear light.
And as for those who have attained to faith in *Allah*[35]
and hold fast to Him—
He will cause them to enter into His compassion
and His abundant blessing,
and guide them to Himself by a straight way.

*Yaa 'ayyuhan nāsu qad jaa'akum burhānum mir-rabbikum
wa 'anzalnaa 'ilayykum nūram mubīnaa.*

*Fa 'ammal lazhīna 'āmanu billāhi
wa'taṣamu bihi
fa sayudkhiluhum fī raḥematim minhu wa faḍlin
wa yahdīhim ilayhi ṣirāṭam mustaqīmaa.*

[4:174–5]

---

[35]The Arabic word for God: used by Arabic speaking Christians as well as Muslims.

The Repast

ʾAl-Māʾidah

Always remember the blessings
which God has bestowed on you,
and the solemn pledge by which He bound you to Himself
when you said, "We have heard, and we pay heed."[36]
And so, remain conscious of God:
truly, God has full knowledge of what is within hearts.

[5:7]

O you who have attained to faith!
Stand firmly in your devotion to God,
bearing witness to the truth in complete fairness;
and never let hatred of anyone
lead you to make the mistake of deviating from justice.
Be just: this is the closest to being God-conscious.
And remain conscious of God:
truly, God is well-aware of all that you do.

[5:8]

---

[36]See also verse 2:285

19

If anyone slays a single soul—
unless it be in punishment for murder
or for spreading corruption on earth—
it shall be as though he had slain all humankind;
whereas, if anyone saves a life,
it shall be as though he had saved the lives of all humanity.

[5:32]

O you who have attained to faith,
remain conscious of God, and seek to come closer to Him,
and strive hard in His cause,
so that you might attain felicity.

Yaa 'ayyuhal lazhīna 'āmanuttaqullāha
wabtaghuu 'ilayhil wasīlata wa jāhidu
fī sabīlihi la'allakum tuflihuun.

[5:35]

And to you We have sent this Book
of the Truth, confirming the truth
of whatever remains of earlier revelations
and guarding what is true within.
Judge in accordance with what God has bestowed from on high,
and do not follow erring views,
forsaking the truth that has come to you.
For every one of you have We designated a law and a way of life.
And if God had so willed,
He could surely have made you all one single community:
but He willed it otherwise in order to test you
by means of what He has bestowed on you.
Strive, then, with one another in doing good!
Your goal is God;
and then, He will make you understand
the truth of everything in which you have differed.

[5:48]

Truly, those who have attained to faith in this Word,
as well as those who follow the Jewish faith,
and the Sabians,[37] and the Christians—
all who have faith in God and the Final Day and do righteous deeds—
no fear need they have,
and neither shall they grieve.

[5:69]

---

[37] Sabians: followers of John the Baptist

O you who have attained to faith!
Do not deprive yourselves of the good things of life
which God has made lawful to you,
but do not transgress the bounds of what is right:
truly, God does not love those who go beyond
the bounds of what is right.
And so partake of the lawful, good things
which God grants you as sustenance,
and be conscious of God, in whom you have faith.

[5:87-88]

On the Day of Reckoning God will say:
"Today, their truthfulness shall benefit
all who have been true to their word.
Theirs shall be gardens through which running waters flow;
there to dwell beyond the count of time;
well-pleased is God with them,
and well-pleased are they with Him: this is the ultimate success."

[5:119]

Cattle

ʾAl-ʾAnʿām

Say, O Prophet: "I do not tell you,
'God's treasures are with me';
nor that I know the things that are beyond
the reach of human perception;
nor do I say to you that I am an angel.
I only follow what is revealed to me."
Say: "Can the blind and the seeing be considered equal?
Then won't you try to understand?"

[6:50]

And warn those who fear
that they shall be gathered to their Sustainer
with none to protect them from Him or to intercede with Him,
so that they might become fully conscious of Him.

And so, do not repulse any of those
who morning and evening call on their Sustainer, seeking His face.
You are in no way accountable for them—
just as they are in no way accountable for you—
and you have no right to repulse them,
for then you would be among those who do harm.

23

For it is in this way that we try them through one another—
so that they might ask, "Is it these among us whom God has favored?"
Does God not know best those who are grateful to Him?
And when those who have faith in our signs come to you,
say: "Peace be with you.
Your Sustainer has willed upon Himself
the law of compassion—
so that if any of you does harm out of ignorance,
and afterwards repents and changes,
Your Sustainer is Ever Ready to Forgive, Most Merciful."

[6:51-4]

For with God are the keys to the Unseen:
the treasures that none knows but He/She.
And He/She knows all that is on the land and in the sea;
and not a leaf falls but He/She knows it;
and neither is there a grain in the earth's deep darkness,
nor anything alive or dead, but is recorded in a clear record.
And He/She it is who causes you to be as dead at night,
and knows what you do during the day;
and each day He/She brings you back to life
so that a term set by Him/Her might be fulfilled.
In the end, to Him/Her you must return;
and He/She will make you understand all that you did.

[6:59-60]

Say: "Truly, God's guidance is the only guidance:
and so we have been called to surrender ourselves
to the Sustainer of all the worlds,
and to be constant in prayer and conscious of Him:
for it is to Him that we shall be gathered together."
And He it is who has created the heavens and the earth
in accordance with an inner truth—
and the Day He says, "Be," it is.
His word is the Truth.
And His will be the dominion
on the Day when the trumpet of resurrection sounds.
He knows all that is beyond the reach of a created being's perception,
as well as all that can be witnessed:
for He alone is Truly Wise, All-Aware.

[6:71-73]

Truly, God is the One who splits the grain and the kernel apart,
bringing forth the living from the dead,
and He/She is the One who brings forth the dead
out of that which is alive.
This then, is God: how then can you be so deluded?
He/She is the One who causes the dawn to break;
and He/She has made the night to be a source of stillness,
and the sun and the moon for reckoning
by the order of the Almighty, the All-knowing.
And He/She it is who has made the stars for you
so that you might be guided by them
through the darknesses of land and sea:
clearly have We detailed Our signs for people of inner knowing.
And He/She it is who has brought you all into being
out of a single soul,
and so designated for each of you a time-limit on earth
and a resting-place after death:
clearly have We detailed Our signs for people who can grasp the truth.

[6:95-98]

Such is God, your Sustainer: there is no god but Hu,[38]
the Creator of everything: then worship Him/Her alone—
for it is He/She who has everything in His/Her care.
No vision can encompass Him/Her,
but He/She encompasses all human vision:
for He/She alone is Subtle Beyond Comprehension, All-Aware.
Means of insight have now come to you
from your Sustainer through this divine Message.
Whoever, then, chooses to see,
does so for the benefit of his/her own soul;
and whoever chooses to remain blind,
does so to his/her own harm.

[6:102-104]

Do not speak ill of those whom others invoke instead of God,
that they might not speak ill of God out of spite and ignorance:
for, We have made their own activities
appear alluring to each community.
In time, to their Sustainer they must return;
and then He will make them understand
the truth of all that they were doing.

[6:108]

---

[38] See note 30.

For it is He who has brought into being gardens—
both the cultivated ones and those growing wild—
and the date-palm, and fields bearing all manner of produce,
and the olive, and the pomegranate:
all resembling one another and yet so different!
Eat of their fruit when it ripens,
and contribute appropriate portions on harvest day.
And do not be wasteful:
truly, He does not love those who are wasteful!

[6:141]

Say, "Come, let me convey to you
what God has prohibited:
"Do not attribute divinity, in any way, to anything beside Him;
be good to your parents;
and do not kill your children out of fear of poverty—
for it is We who shall provide sustenance
for you as well as for them;
and do not incline towards any shameful deeds,
whether openly or in secret;
and do not take the life of a single soul—
which God has declared sacred—
except out of justice: this has He instructed you
that you might learn wisdom.
And do not touch the substance of an orphan—
except to improve it—before he comes of age."
And give full measure and weigh equitably:
no burden do We place on any soul,
but that which it can bear;
and when you speak, speak justly,
even if a near relative is concerned;
and always observe your bond with God:
this has He asked of you, that you might remember.
And this is the way leading straight to Me:
follow it, then, and do not follow other ways,
that they might not cause you to wander from His way.
This has He asked of you,
so that you might remain conscious of Him.

[6:151-3]

Say: "Truly, my Instructor has guided me
onto a straight way through a steadfast faith—
the way of Abraham, the true one,
who was not of those who attribute divinity to anything beside God."
Say: "Truly, my prayer, and all my acts of worship,
and my living and my dying are for God alone,
the Sustainer of all worlds."

Qul ʾinnanī hadānī rabbee
ʾilā ṣirāṭim mustaqīmin dīnan qiyyamam
millata ʾIbrāhīma ḥanīfaa.
Wa mā kāna minal mushrikeen.

Qul ʾinna ṣalātī wa nusukī
wa maḥeyyāya wa mamātī lillāhi
rabbil ʿālameen.

[6:161–162]

It is He who has made you His representatives on earth:
He has raised you in ranks, some above others,
that He may test you with the gifts He has given
for your Sustainer is swift with stringency,
yet Ever Ready to Forgive, Infinitely Merciful.

[6:165]

30

The Faculty of Discernment

ʾAl-ʾAʿrāf

O children of Adam!
Indeed, We have given you garments to cover your nakedness,
and as a thing of beauty;
but the garment of God consciousness is the best of all.
This is one of God's messages—
that human beings might take it to heart.

[7:26]

Say: "My Sustainer has but urged the doing of what is right;
and He/She wants you to put your whole being
into every act of worship,
and to call Him/Her, sincere in your faith in Him/Her alone.
As it was He/She who brought you into being in the beginning,
so also to Him/Her will you return."

[7:29]

O children of Adam! Beautify yourselves for every act of worship,
and eat and drink, but do not waste:
truly, He does not love the wasteful!

[7:31]

Those who have attained to faith and do righteous deeds—
and We do not burden any soul
with more than it is well able to bear—
they will be companions of the Garden, there to dwell,
after We shall have removed whatever unworthy thoughts or feelings
may have been lingering in their hearts.
Running waters will flow at their feet;
and they will say: "All praise belongs to God, Who has guided us here;
for certainly we would not have found the right path
unless God were our guide!
Truly, our Sustainer's messengers have told us the truth!"
And a voice will call out to them:
"This is the Garden which by virtue of your deeds has come to you."

[7:42-43]

Call to your Sustainer humbly, and in the secrecy of your hearts.
Truly, He does not love those who go beyond the bounds
of what is right.
And so, do not spread corruption on earth
after it has been so well ordered.
And call to Him with awe and longing:
truly, God's grace is very near those who do good.
And He it is who sends the winds
as joyous news of His coming grace—
so that, when they have brought heavy clouds
We may drive them towards dead land and cause rain to descend;
that by it We may cause all manner of fruitfulness to spring forth.
Even so shall We cause the dead to emerge—
perhaps you will remember.

[7:55-57]

"Establish for us what is good in this world
as well as in the life to come:
see how we have turned to You in repentance!"
God answered: "With My stringency I try whom I will—
but My mercy overspreads everything,
and so I shall confer it upon those who are conscious of Me
and spend in charity, and who have faith in Our signs."

[7:156]

It is He who has created you all out of one soul,
and out of it brought into being a mate,
so that man might incline with love towards woman.
And so, when he has embraced her, she conceives a light burden,
and continues to bear it.
Then, when she grows heavy, they both pray to God, their Sustainer:
"If You grant us a righteous child,
we shall most certainly be among the grateful."

[7:189]

Make due allowance for human nature,
and urge the doing of what is right;
and leave alone all those who choose to remain ignorant.

[7:199]

And yet, when you do not produce a sign for them,
some say, "why don't you seek to obtain it from God?"
Say: "I only follow whatever is revealed to me by my Sustainer:
this revelation is a means of insight from your Sustainer,
and a guidance and grace to those who will have faith.
And so when the Qurʾān is voiced, pay attention to it,
and listen in silence, so that you might be graced with God's mercy."
And remember your Sustainer humbly within yourself and with awe,
and without raising your voice,
in the morning and in the evening;
and don't allow yourself to be unaware.

See how those who are near to your Sustainer
are never too proud to worship Him;
and they praise His limitless glory,
and prostrate themselves before Him alone.

[7:203-6]

Spoils of War

ʾAl-ʾAnfāl

The faithful are those
whose hearts tremble with awe whenever God is mentioned,
and whose faith is strengthened
whenever His signs are conveyed to them,
and who place their trust in their Sustainer—
those who are constant in prayer
and spend on others out of what We provide for them as sustenance:
In truth, these are the faithful!
They shall have stations of dignity with their Sustainer,
and forgiveness, and a most generous provision.

[8:2-4]

Yes! You were praying to your Sustainer for help,
and then He responded to you:
"Truly, I shall aid you with a thousand angels
following one after another!"
And God conferred this solely as a glad tiding,
that by it your hearts should be set at rest—
since no help can come from any but God:
truly, God is Almighty, Wise!
Remember how it was when He caused inner calm to enfold you,
as an assurance from Him,
and sent down over you water from the skies
so that by it He might purify you
and free you from the unclean whisperings of Satan
and strengthen your hearts and so make your steps firm.
Witness! Your Sustainer inspired the angels
to convey His message to the faithful:
"I am with you!"

[8:9-12]

O you who have faith!
Respond to the call of God and the messenger
whenever he calls you to that which will give you life;
and know that God intervenes between man and his desires,
and that you shall be gathered back to Him.

[8:24]

O you who have attained to faith!
If you remain conscious of God,
He will endow you with a standard by which to discern
the true from the false,
and will clear evil from you,
and will forgive you your mistakes:
for God is limitless in the abundance of His blessing.

[8:29]

God would never change the blessings
with which He has graced a people
unless they change their inner selves;
and, truly, God is All-Hearing, All-Seeing.

[8:53]

Repentance

'At-Tawbah

And God does not grace with guidance
people who deliberately do wrong.
Those who have faith
and who have turned away from evil
and who strive hard in God's cause
with their possessions and their lives
have the highest rank in God's sight,
and it is they who shall attain!
Their Sustainer gives them the glad tiding
of the grace that flows from Him,
and of His abundant acceptance,
and of the gardens which await them, of enduring bliss,
there to dwell forever.
Truly, in God's Presence is a mighty recompense!

[9:19-22]

As for the faithful, both men and women—
they are protectors of one another:
they urge the doing of what is right
and forbid the doing of what is wrong,
and are constant in prayer, and render the charity that purifies,
and they heed God and His messenger.
It is they on whom God will bestow His blessing:
truly, God is Almighty, Truly Wise!
God has promised the faithful, both men and women,
gardens beneath which running waters flow, there to abide
and fair dwellings in gardens of enduring bliss;
but God's good acceptance is the greatest bliss of all—
for this is the ultimate success!

[9:71-72]

See how God has purchased of the faithful
their lives and their possessions;
in return, theirs is the Garden,
and so they struggle in God's way.

[9:111]

O you who have attained to faith!
Remain conscious of God,
and be among those who are true to their word!

*Yaa ʾayyuhal lazhīna ʾāmanut taqullāha
wa kūnū maʿaṣ ṣādiqeen.*

[9:119]

39

Jonah

Yunus

Truly, those who have faith and do righteous deeds
their Sustainer will guide by means of their faith:
beneath them will flow rivers in Gardens of Bliss.
There they will call out:
"Glory to You, O God!"
and they will be answered with the greeting, "Peace!"
And the completion of their cry will be:
"Praise be to God, the Cherisher and Sustainer of all the Worlds!"

*'Innal lazhīna 'āmanu wa 'amiluṣ ṣāliḥāti
yaḥdīhim rabbuhum bi 'īmānihim,
tajrī min taḥtihimul 'anhāru fī jannātin naʿeem.*

*Daʿwāhum fīhā subeḥānakal lāhumma
wa taḥiyyatuhum fīhā salaam.
Wa 'ākhiru daʿwāhum 'anil ḥamdu lillāhi
rabbil ʿālameen.*

[10:9-10]

The parable of the life of this world is as the rain
which We send down from the skies—
absorbed by the earth, it encourages plants to spring forth
which provide nourishment for humans and animals;
until the earth is adorned with its golden ornaments
and is enhanced,
so that those who dwell on it
may think they have gained mastery over it;
but by night or by day, Our Command reaches it,
and We make it become like a clear-cut field
as if only the day before it had not flourished!
And so We explain the signs in detail for those who reflect.
But God invites to the Abode of Peace;
He guides those that will to a way that is straight.
To those who do good is a good recompense, even more!
No darkness nor shame will veil their faces!
They are companions of the Garden; there will they dwell!

[10:24-26]

O humankind! there has come to you a direction from your Lord
and a healing for your hearts
and for those who have faith, guidance and grace.
Say: "In the abundance of God and in His grace,
in that let them rejoice;
that is better than whatever they may hoard."

[10:57-58]

And whatever you may endeavor,
and whatever portion you may be reciting from the Qur'ān,
and whatever deed you may be doing,
We are Witnesses of it when you enter into it.
For not even the weight of an atom on the earth or in heaven
is beyond the awareness of Your Sustainer.
And there is neither the least nor the greatest of these things
but are clearly recorded.
See: truly, with the friends of God
there is no fear nor shall they grieve;
those who have faith and constantly guard against evil,
for them are glad tidings in the present life
and in the life to come:
no alteration can there be in the Words of God.
This is indeed the ultimate prosperity.

[10:61-64]

And Moses said, "O my people!
If you have faith in God, place your trust in Him—
if you have truly surrendered yourselves to Him!"

[10:84]

Hud[39]

See how they fold up their hearts that they might hide from Him!
But even when they cover themselves with their garments
He knows all that they conceal
and what they disclose:
for He knows well what is within hearts.
There is no living creature on earth
but its sustenance depends on God;
He knows its term and where it makes its home;
everything is clearly recorded.
It is He Who created the heavens and the earth in six aeons
and the Throne of His power rested on the waters
that He might test you as to which of you is best in conduct.

[11:5-7]

---

[39] *Hud* was one of the prophets of the Abrahamic tradition. Said to have been the
first Arabian prophet, he was of the tribe of 'Ad which occupied the extensive
desert region known as *Al-Aqhaf*. Though for a time the tribe of 'Ad was
extremely powerful and influential, it later vanished.

If We give a person a taste of mercy from Ourselves
and then take it from him,
see how he falls into despair and is ungrateful.
But if We give him a taste of grace
after hardship has come to him
he is sure to say, "All affliction has left me;"
and witness, how proudly he triumphs.
But not those who patiently persevere
and do good deeds;
for them is forgiveness and a great reward.

[11:9-11]

"I don't say to you that with me are the Treasures of God
nor that I know what is beyond human perceiving
nor do I claim to be an angel.
Nor yet do I say of those whom your eyes despise
that God will not grant them that which is good;
God knows best what is within their souls.
If I did so I should indeed be of those who do wrong."

(Words of Noah)

[11:31]

"And O my people! ask forgiveness of your Sustainer
and turn to Him in repentance.
From the heavens He will pour down abundant rain upon you
and add strength to your strength;
so do not turn back in error!"

(Words of Hūd)

[11:52]

To the Madyan people We sent Shu'ayb one of their own.
He said: "O my people! worship God: you have no other god but Him.
And don't give short measure or weigh lightly;
I see you prosper now, but I dread that suffering may befall you
on an all-encompassing Day.
And O my people! measure and weigh justly
and don't deprive people of what is rightfully theirs;
and don't act wickedly on earth, spreading corruption.
That which rests with God is best for you if you would only have faith!
Yet, I am not meant to stand guard over you!"

[11:4–86]

"But ask forgiveness of your Sustainer
and turn to Him:
for truly, my Sustainer is infinitely merciful and loving."

(Words of Shu'ayb)

[11:90]

And be constant in prayer at both ends of the day
and at the coming of the night,
for good deeds repel those that are evil.
Let this be a reminder to those who remember God.

[11:114]

All that We relate to you of the stories of the messengers,
with it We strengthen your heart:
for through these Truth comes to you
as well as counsel
and a message of remembrance to those who have faith.

[11:120]

Joseph

Yusuf

"Truly, none but those who deny the truth
ever lose hope of God's life-giving mercy."

[12:86]

"O my Sustainer!
You have indeed bestowed on me some power,
and have imparted to me some knowledge
of the inner meaning of that which occurs.
Originator of the heavens and the earth!
You are my Protector in this world
and in the life to come:
let me die as one who has surrendered himself to You,
and unite me with the righteous!"

(Joseph's prayer)

Rabbi qad ʾātaytanī minal mulki
wa ʿalamtanī min taʾwīlil ʾaḥādeeth.
Fāṭiras samāwāti wal ʾarḍi
ʾanta waliyyī fid dunyā wal ʾākhirati
tawaffanī musliman wa ʾalḥiqnī biṣ ṣāliḥeen

[12:101]

Say: "This is my way:
based on understanding through conscious insight,
I am calling to God—
I and those who follow me."
And say: "Limitless is God in His glory;
and never will I be of those who attribute divinity
to anything beside Him!"

Qul hāzhihi sabīlee ʾadʿuu ʾilallaah.
ʿAlā baṣīratin ʾanā wa manittabaʿanī
wa subḥānallāhi wa maa ʾanā
minal mushrikeen.

[12:108]

Thunder

ʾAr-Raʿd

Truly, God will never change the condition of a people
unless they change their inner selves.
But when God wills a people to suffer reproach none can avert it,
nor will they find any protector other than God.
It is He Who displays before you the lightning
to engender both fear and hope;
it is He Who raises up the clouds heavy with rain,
and the thunder repeats His praises and so do the angels with awe;
He lets loose the thunderbolts
and strikes with them whom He wills.
Yet they stubbornly dispute about God,
though His alone is the power to complete His will!
To Him alone belong all prayers towards Truth.
Any others that they invoke besides Him
hear them no more than if they were to stretch forth their hands
for water to reach their mouths but it falls short;
for the prayer of those without faith is nothing but futile wandering.
Whatever beings exist in the heavens and the earth
prostrate themselves to God willingly or unwillingly,
as do their shadows in the mornings and evenings.

[13:11-15]

Say: "God is the Creator of all things;
He is the One, the Supreme, the Irresistible."
He sends down water from the skies and the channels flow,
each according to its measure;
but the water carries away the foam that mounts to the surface.
Even so from that which they smelt in the fire
to make ornaments or utensils, scum surfaces.
And so God reveals Truth and vanity:
for the scum disappears like discarded froth,
while that which is for the good of humanity remains on the earth.
And so God offers parables.
In store for those who respond to their Sustainer is the ultimate good.

[13:16-18]

Those who are true to their bond with God
and do not fail in their pledge;
those who keep together what God has commanded to be joined,
and stand in awe of their Sustainer and the awesome reckoning to come;
those who patiently persevere seeking the Face of their Sustainer,
and are constant in prayer,
who distribute secretly and openly
from what We have given them for their sustenance,
and turn away evil with good:
for these is the fulfillment of the ultimate Abode—
gardens of endless bliss—which they shall enter
together with the righteous among their parents,
their spouses, and their offspring,
and angels shall greet them from every gate:
"Peace be with you for having patiently persevered!
Then how excellent is the final dwelling-place!"

[13:21-24]

He guides to Himself all who turn to Him—
those who have faith
and whose hearts find satisfaction in the remembrance of God—

for, truly, in the remembrance of God hearts find rest.

'Alā bizhikril-lāhi taṭma'innul quluub.

[13:28]

For each period is a Book.
God annuls or confirms what He pleases—
for with Him is the Mother of the Book.
Whether We shall show you while you are living
some of what We promised them
or take your soul to Ourselves before it is fulfilled,
your duty is only to convey the Message;
Ours is the reckoning.

[13:39-40]

Abraham

ʾIbrāhīm

Alif Lam Ra.[40]
A book We have revealed to you
so that you might bring forth all humankind,
by their Sustainer's blessing,
out of the depths of darkness into the light:
onto the way of the Almighty,
the One to whom all praise belongs.

[14:1]

And, indeed, We sent forth Moses with Our signs:
"Lead your people out of the depths of darkness into the light,
and remind them of the Days of God!"
Truly, in this there are signs
for all who patiently persevere and are deeply grateful to God.

[14:5]

---

[40] The mystical letters: Preceding about a quarter of the Qur'anic *surahs* are combinations of letters sometimes referred to as "openings" (*fawatih*). They are always pronounced individually. Though various theories as to their meaning exist, their true meaning rests in the Mysterion. As Abu-Bakr, close companion of the Prophet and the first of the Caliphs to guide his community after his passing said, "In every Divine Book there is mystery—and the mystery of the Qur'an is indicated in the openings of some of the *surahs*.

Those who have faith and do righteous deeds
will be brought into gardens beneath which running waters flow,
there to dwell by their Sustainers consent,
and will be welcomed with the greeting, "Peace!"
Are you not aware how God offers the parable of a good word?
It is like a good tree, firmly rooted,
reaching its branches towards the sky,
always yielding fruit, by consent of its Sustainer.
This is how God offers parables to human beings,
so that they might consider the truth.
And the parable of a corrupt word is that of a corrupt tree,
torn up from its roots onto the surface of the earth,
unable to endure.
Even so God grants firmness to those who have come to faith
through the word that is unshakably true,
in this world as well as in the life to come.

[14:23-27]

And remember that it is God who has created the heavens and the earth,
and who sends down rain from the sky
and by it brings forth all kind of fruits for your provision;
and who has made ships in service to you,
so that they may sail through the sea at His command;
and has made the rivers in service to you;
and has made the sun and the moon,
both of them constant in their courses,
in service to His laws, so that they may be of use to you;
and has made the night and the day in service to you.

And always does He give you something
out of what you may be asking of Him,
and if you tried to count God's blessings,
you could never compute them.

[14:32-34]

And remember the time when Abraham spoke:
"O my Sustainer! Make this land secure,
and preserve me and my children from ever worshipping idols—
for, truly, O my Sustainer, these have led many people astray!
So only the one who follows me in this faith is truly of me;
and as for the one who acts against me—
You are, truly, Always Ready to Forgive, Most Merciful!
O my Sustainer! Witness, I have settled some of my offspring
in a valley without arable land, close to Your Sacred House,[41]
so that, O our Sustainer, they might devote themselves to prayer:
so cause people's hearts to open towards them,
and grant them fruitful sustenance, so that they might be grateful.
O our Sustainer! Truly, You know all that we may hide in our hearts
as well as all that we may disclose:
for nothing whatever, be it on earth or in heaven, is hidden from God.
All praise belongs to God, who has granted me, in my old age,
Ishmael and Isaac! Witness,
truly, my Sustainer is the One who hears all prayer:
so, O my Sustainer, cause me and some of my offspring
to remain constant in prayer!

And, O our Sustainer, accept this my prayer:
Grant Your forgiveness to me, and my parents, and all the faithful,
on the Day on which the last reckoning will come to pass."

Rabbanāghfir lī wa liwālidayya wa lil muʾminīna
yawma yaqūmul ḥisaab.

[14:35-41]

---

[41] The Kaʾ bah which is located in a desert valley.

55

ʾAl-Ḥijr[42]

And We have spread the earth out wide;
set upon it firm and immovable mountains;
and produced upon it all kinds of things in balance.
And We have provided there means of subsistence for you
and for those whose provision does not depend on you.
And there is not a thing but its storehouses are with Us;
but We only send it down in appropriate measures.
And We send the fertilizing winds,
then cause the rain to descend from the sky
and so provide you with water
though you are not the guardians of its stores.
And, truly, it is We Who give life and who give death:
it is We Who shall remain after all else passes away.
To Us are known those of you who hasten forward
and those who lag behind.
Surely, it is your Sustainer Who will gather them together;
for He is All-Wise and All-Knowing.

[15:19-25]

---

[42] *Al-Ḥijr:* the rocky region in the northern *Hijaz* which was in pre-Islamic times occupied by the tribe of *Thamud.* From among them the prophet *Salih* was called forth to counsel his people who had become arrogant and corrupt in their prosperity.

The Bee

'An-Naḥl

And cattle He has created for you:
from them you derive warmth and numerous benefits
and of them you eat.
And you have a sense of pride and beauty in them
as you drive them home in the evening
and as you lead them forth to pasture in the morning.
And they carry your heavy loads
to lands that you could not reach
except with great hardship to yourselves:
truly, your Sustainer is indeed Infinitely Compassionate, Most Merciful.
And He creates horses and mules and asses for you to ride,
as well as for beauty;
He will yet create things of which you have no knowledge.

And to God leads straight the Way
but there are ways that turn aside:
if God had willed He could have guided all of you.
It is He Who sends down rain from the sky:
from it you drink and with it plants grow
on which you feed your cattle.
With it He produces for you grain, olives,
date-palms, grapes, and all kinds of fruit:
truly, in this is a sign for people who reflect.
He has made in service to you the night and the day
and the sun and the moon;
the stars, too, are in service by His Command:
truly, in this are signs for those who are wise.

And the things on this earth
which He has multiplied in varying hues:
truly, in this is a sign
for those who celebrate the praises of God.
It is He Who has made the sea in service
that you may eat from it flesh that is fresh and tender
and that you may extract from it ornaments to wear;
and you see the ships that break across its waves
that you may seek of the bounty of God
and that you may be grateful.
And He has set upon the earth
mountains standing firm lest it should shake with you;
and rivers and roads, that you may guide yourselves,
and signs and means of orientation;
for by the stars men find their way.
Is then He Who creates like one who cannot create?
Will you not listen to counsel?
If you were to count the favors of God
never would you be able to compute them:
for God is Oft-Forgiving, Most Merciful.

[16:5-18]

And We sent down the Book to you
that you might make clear to them those things in which they differ
and that it should be a guide and a mercy to those who have faith.
And God sends down rain from the skies
and with it bestows life to the earth that was dead:
truly, in this is a sign for those who pay attention.
And also in cattle you will find an instructive sign.
From what is within their bodies between excretions and blood
We produce for you pure milk, pleasing to those who drink it.
And from the fruit of the date–palm and the vine
you obtain nourishing food and drink:
witness, in this, also, is a sign for those who are wise.
And your Sustainer taught the bee to build its cells
in hills, on trees, and in dwelling places,
then to eat of all that the earth produces
and to skillfully find the spacious paths of its Lord.
There issues from within their bodies a drink of varied hues
containing healing for human beings:
truly, in this is a sign for those who reflect.

[16: 64-69]

God commands justice, the doing of good,
and generosity to your relatives
and He forbids all shameful deeds and injustice and rebellion;
He instructs you so that you may receive counsel.
Fulfill the bond with God when you have entered into it
and do not break your oaths after you have confirmed them;
indeed you have made God your assurance;
for God knows all that you do.
And don't be like a woman who breaks into untwisted strands
the yarn that she has spun after it has been strengthened.
Nor take oaths to deceive between yourselves
lest one group should be more numerous than another;
for God will test you by this,
and on the Day of Reckoning He will certainly make clear to you
the truth of all that about which you disagree.

[16:90-92]

Do not sell the bond with God for a miserable price:
for that which is with God is by far the best for you if only you knew.
What is with you must vanish; what is with God will endure.
And We will certainly bestow on those who patiently persevere
their reward according to the best of their actions.
Whoever works righteousness, man or woman, and has faith,
truly, to him/her will We give a new life, a life that is good and pure,
and We will bestow on such their recompense
according to the best of their actions.

[16:95-96]

60

But, truly, your Sustainer, to those who do wrong in ignorance
but who afterwards repent and make amends,
your Sustainer after all this is Most Ready to Forgive, Most Merciful.

[16:119]

Abraham was a man who combined within himself all virtues,
devoutly obedient to God, and true in faith,
and he did not attribute divinity to anything beside God;
he was always grateful for the blessings of God
Who chose him and guided him to a straight way.
And We gave him good in this world
and he will be in the Hereafter in the ranks of the righteous.
So We have inspired you:
"Follow the ways of Abraham, who turned away from all that is false,
and who did not join other gods with God."

[16:120-123]

Invite to the way of your Lord with wisdom and beautiful urging;
and discuss with them in the best and most gracious manner
for your Lord knows best who strays from His Path
and who receives guidance.
And if you do engage expose them,
respond to them no worse than they respond to you;
but if you show patience that is indeed best for those who are patient.
Then be patient, always remembering that your patience is from God;
and do not grieve over them;
and do not worry yourself because of their plots.
For God is with those who restrain themselves
and those who do good.

[16:125-128]

The Night Journey

ʾAl-ʾIsrāʾ

Limitless in His glory is He who transported His servant by night
from the Inviolable House of Worship[43]
to the Remote House of Worship[44]—
the surroundings of which We had blessed—
so that We might show him some of Our symbols:
for, truly, He alone is All-Hearing, All-Seeing.
And We granted revelation to Moses,
and made it a guidance for the children of Israel:
"Do not attribute to any but Me the power to determine your fate,
O descendants of those whom We caused to be carried with Noah!
Witness, he was a most grateful servant!"

[17:1-3]

---

[43]Inviolable House of Worship signifies the Kaʿbah in Mecca.
[44]Remote House of Worship signifies the Masjidul-Aqsā in Jerusalem. The night of
the spiritual ascent of Muḥammad, he was transported by Gabriel from Mecca to
Jerusalem. From there he mounted his steed Burāq, and rising to the seventh
heaven, ascended alone from there to within "two-bow lengths" of God's Throne.

As it is, human beings often pray for things that are harmful
as if they were praying for that which is good:
for people are inclined to be hasty.
And We have established the night and the day as two symbols;
and then We have effaced the symbol of night
and put in place the light-giving symbol of day,
so that you might seek to obtain your Sustainer's bounty
and be aware of the passing years and of the reckoning.
For clearly, most clearly, have We spelled out everything!
And every human being's destiny have we bound to his neck;
and on the Day of Reckoning
We shall bring forth for him a record which he will find wide open:
"Read this, your record!
Your own self is sufficient today to discern your account!"
Whoever chooses to follow the right path,
follows it but for his own good;
and whoever goes astray, goes but astray to his own hurt;
and no bearer of burdens shall be made to bear another's burden.
And never would We chastise before sending a Messenger.

[17:11-15]

Do not join any other deity side by side with God,
that you might not find yourself disgraced and in want:
for your Sustainer has commanded
that you shall worship none but Him.
And do good to your parents.
Should one of them, or both, reach old age in your care,
never speak with contempt to them or scold them,
but speak to them with reverence,
and tenderly lower to them the wings of humility,
and say: "O my Sustainer! Bestow Your grace upon them,
even as they cherished and nurtured me when I was but a child!"

[17: 22-24]

And give their due to your close relations,
as well as to the needy and the traveler,
but do not squander senselessly.
Witness, those who squander are truly like satans—
for Satan has indeed proved most ungrateful to his Sustainer.
And if you must turn aside from those seeking
to obtain your Sustainer's grace and hoping for it,
at least speak to them gently,
and neither allow your hand to be chained to your neck,
nor stretch it forth to your utmost limit,
that you might not find yourself blamed, or even destitute.
Witness, your Sustainer grants abundant sustenance,
or gives it in scant measure, to whomever He wills:
truly, He is completely aware of His creatures, and sees them all.

[17:26-30]

And so, do not kill your children for fear of poverty:
it is We who shall provide sustenance for them as well as for you.
Truly, killing them is a great sin.
And do not approach adultery—
for, behold, it is an abomination and an evil way.
And do not take any human being's life—
which God has willed to be sacred—
except in the pursuit of justice.

[17:31-33]

And do not touch the substance of an orphan,
except to improve it, before he comes of age.
And be true to every promise—
for, truly, you will be called to account for every promise
which you will have made!
And give full measure whenever you measure,
and weigh with a balance that is true:
this will be for your own good, and best in the end.
And never concern yourself
with anything of which you have no knowledge;
truly, hearing and sight and heart—all of them—
will be called to account for it!
And do not walk upon the earth with proud self-conceit:
for, truly, you can never rend the earth asunder,
nor can you ever grow as tall as the mountains!
The evil of all this is odious in your Sustainer's sight:
this is part of that knowledge of right and wrong
with which your Sustainer has inspired you.

[17:34-38]

Limitless is He in His glory,
and sublimely, immeasurably exalted
above anything people may say.
The seven heavens acclaim His limitless glory,
and the earth, and all that they contain;
and there is nothing that does not celebrate His immeasurable glory—
but you fail to grasp the manner of their glorifying Him!
Truly, He is forbearing, always ready to forgive!

[17:44]

Be constant in your prayer
from the time when the sun has passed its zenith
until the darkness of night,
and always be mindful of its recitation at dawn:
for see how the recitation at dawn
is indeed witnessed by all that is holy.
And rise from your sleep and pray during part of the night,
as a free offering,
and your Sustainer may well raise you to a glorious station.
And say: "O my Sustainer!
Cause me to enter upon whatever I may do in a true and sincere way,
and cause me to complete it in a true and sincere way,
and grant me, out of Your grace, sustaining strength!"
And say: "Truth has now arrived,
and falsehood has withered away:
for, witness, all falsehood is bound to wither away!"

[17:78-81]

Say: "Invoke God,
or invoke the Most Gracious:
by whichever name you invoke Him/Her,[45]
His/Hers are all the attributes of perfection."
And do not be too loud in your prayer
nor speak it in too low a voice, but follow a middle way.

[17:110]

---

[45] See Note on Translation, p. XV and note 30.

The Cave

'Al-Kahf

That which is on earth
We have made but as a glittering show for the earth
in order that We may test them
as to which of them are best in conduct.

[18:7]

When those youths took refuge in the cave,
they prayed,

"O our Sustainer!
Bestow on us Your grace
and endow us, whatever our condition,
with consciousness of what is right!"

*Rabbanaa 'ātinā mil ladunka raḥmatan
wa ḥayyi' lanā min 'amrinā rashadaa.*

[18:10]

Do not say of anything "I shall be sure to do so and so tomorrow"
without adding "If God wills!"
And call your Sustainer to mind when you forget,
and say: "I hope that my Lord will guide me
ever closer even than this to the right path."

Wa lā taqūlanna lishay'in 'innī fā'ilun zhālika ghadan
'Illaa 'an yashaa 'Allaah!
Wazhekur rabbaka 'izhā nasīta
wa qul 'asaa 'an yahdiyani Rabbī
li 'aqraba min hāzhā rashadaa.

[18:23-24]

With Him are the secrets of the heavens and the earth:
how clearly He sees; how finely He hears!
They have no protector other than Him;
nor does He share His Command with anyone.
And speak what has been revealed to you of the Book of your Lord:
nothing can change His Words
and you will find no refuge other than Him.
And keep your soul content with those
who call on their Sustainer morning and evening seeking His Face;
and do not let your eyes pass beyond them
seeking the fame and glitter of this life;
nor obey any whose heart
We have permitted to neglect the remembrance of Us—
one who follows his own desires and has gone beyond all bounds.
Say: "The Truth is from your Lord."
As to those who have faith and work righteousness,
Truly, We shall not allow to perish
the recompense of anyone who does a good deed.

[18:26-30]

The only protection comes from God, the True One.
He is the Best to reward and the Best to give success.

Hunālikal walāyatu lillāhil Ḥaqq.
Hūwa khayrun thawāban wa khayrun ʿuqbaa.

[18:44]

Say: "If the sea were ink for the words of my Sustainer
the sea would be used up sooner
than would the words of my Sustainer,
even if we added to it sea upon sea."

[18:109]

Mary

Maryam

And call to mind through this Book, Mary—
she withdrew from her family to an eastern place
and kept herself in seclusion from them;
then We sent to her Our angel, and he appeared before her
in the shape of a well-made human being.
She said, "I seek refuge from you with the Most Gracious:
do not come near me if you stand in awe of Him."
He said, "I am only a messenger from your Sustainer,
who says, 'I shall bestow upon you a holy son.' "
She said, "How can I have a son when no man has ever touched me,
and I am chaste?"
He said, "So it is; your Sustainer says, 'This is easy for me,
and so that We might make him a sign for human beings
and a Mercy from Us':
it was a thing decreed."

[19:16-21]

Those who repent and have faith and work righteousness:
these will enter the Garden, and will not be wronged in any way—
Gardens of Eternity, those which the Most Gracious
has promised to His servants in the Unseen:
for His promise must be fulfilled.
They will not hear any empty talk there
but only greetings of peace;
and there they will receive their sustenance, morning and evening.
Such is the Garden which We bestow as an inheritance
to those of Our Servants who are conscious of Us.
(The angels say:) "We descend by command of your Sustainer alone:
to Him belongs what lies open before us
and what is behind us and what is between;
and your Sustainer never forgets,
the Sustainer of the heavens and of the earth
and of all that is between them.
So worship Him and be constant and patient in His worship:
do you know of any whose name is worthy
to be mentioned side by side with His?"

[19:60-65]

"And God endows with an ever-deeper consciousness of the right way
those who seek guidance;
and good deeds, the fruits of which endure forever,
are best in the sight of your Sustainer
and yield the best return."

[19:76]

72

Truly, those who have faith and do righteous deeds
will the Most Gracious endow with Love.

*Innal lazhīna 'āmanu wa 'amiluṣ ṣāliḥāti
sayaf'alu lahumur-Raḥmānu wuddaa.*

[19:96]

O Humankind

Ṭa-Hā

We have not sent down the Qurʾān to you to distress you
but only as a counsel to those who stand in awe of God,
a revelation from Him Who created the earth and the high heavens;
the Most Gracious is firmly established on the throne of authority.
To Him belongs what is in the heavens and on earth
and all between them and all beneath the soil.
Whether you pronounce the word aloud or not,
truly, He knows what is secret and what is yet more hidden.
God! there is no god but Hu![46]
To Him belong the Most Beautiful Names.

[20:1-8]

Moses said: "O my Sustainer! expand for me my breast;
ease my task for me;
and remove the impediment from my speech
so they may understand what I say;
and give me a helper from my family,
Aaron, my brother;
add to my strength through him
and make him share my task
that we may celebrate Your praise continually
and remember You unceasingly:
for You are He Who watches over us."
God said: "All that you ask for is granted, O Moses!"

[20:25-36]

---

[46] See note 30.

"Eat of the good things We have provided for your sustenance
but not to excess so that My Wrath might not descend on you:
for those on whom My Wrath descends
have thrown themselves into ruin!
"But without doubt I am the One Who forgives again and again
those who repent, have faith, and do right,
those who turn to receive true guidance."

[20:81-82]

Hu[47] knows all that is before them and all that is hidden from them,
but they cannot encompass Him with their knowledge.
All faces shall be humbled
before the Ever-Living, the Self-Subsisting, the Eternal:
hopeless indeed will be the one who carries corruption,
but the one who acts rightly and has faith
need have no fear of harm nor of any lessening of what is due him/her.
And so we have sent down this, an Arabic Qurʾān,
and explained in it in detail some of the warnings
so that they may stand in awe of God
or that it may cause remembrance in them.
High above all is God, the Sovereign, the Truth!
Do not be hasty with the Qurʾān
before its revelation to you is complete,
but say: "O my Sustainer! Increase my knowing."

[20:110-114]

---

[47] See note 30.

And so be patient with what they say
and celebrate the praises of your Sustainer
before the rising of the sun and before its setting;
yes, celebrate them for part of the hours of the night
and at the edges of the day: that you may have felicity.
Nor strain your eyes in longing
for the things We have given for enjoyment to some of them—
the splendor of the life of this world through which We test them—
for the provision of your Sustainer is better and more enduring.
Encourage prayer in your people and be constant within it.
We are not asking you to provide sustenance:
We provide it for you.
But the fruit of the Hereafter is for the vigilant.

[20:130-132]

The Prophets

ʾAl-ʾAmbiyāʾ

In the past We granted to Moses and Aaron the Criterion
and a Light and a Message for those who would do right,
those who stand in awe of their Sustainer in their most secret thoughts
and who hold in awe the Hour of Reckoning.
And this is a Message of blessing which We have sent down:
will you then reject it?

[21:48-50]

And remember David and Solomon
when they gave judgment concerning the field
into which the sheep of certain people had strayed by night:
We witnessed their judgment.
In Solomon We inspired the understanding of the matter;
to each We gave Judgment and Knowledge;
it was Our power that made the hills
and the birds celebrate Our praises with David;
it was We Who did these things.
It was We Who taught him the making of protective garments
for your benefit to fortify you against all that might cause you fear;
but are you grateful?

[21:78-80]

And remember Job when he cried out to his Sustainer:
"Truly, affliction has seized me,
but You are the Most Merciful of those who are merciful."
So We listened to him: We removed his distress
and We restored his people to him, doubling their number
as a Grace from Ourselves
and as a remembrance for all who serve Us.

[21:83-84]

Truly, this community of yours is one community
and I am your Sustainer:
therefore serve Me alone.

*'Inna hāzhihi 'ummatukum 'ummatan wāḥidatan
wa 'anā rabbukumfa'buduun.*

[21:92]

And indeed, after the reminding, we wrote in all the books of wisdom:
"My righteous servants shall inherit the earth."
Truly, in this is a Message
for people who would worship God.
We have sent you as a grace for all creatures.
Say: "What has come to me by inspiration is that your God is One God:
will you then surrender yourselves to Him?"

[21:106-108]

The Pilgrimage

ʾAl-Ḥajj

O humankind! If you are doubtful about the resurrection—
truly, We have created you out of dust,
then out of a drop of sperm,
then out of a joining, then out of an evolving embryo,
so that We might make it clear to you.
And We cause whom We will to rest in the womb
for a determined time,
and then We bring you forth as infants and
so that some of you might attain to maturity:
for some among you are caused to die in childhood,
just as many of you are diminished in old age to a most abject state,
ceasing to know anything they once knew so well.
And you can see the earth dry and lifeless—
and suddenly, when We send down waters upon it,
it stirs and swells and sprouts forth every kind of lovely plant!
All this happens because God alone is the Ultimate Truth,
and because He alone brings the dead to life,
and because He has the power to will anything.

[22:5-6]

For, when We assigned to Abraham the site of this Temple,[48]
We said to him: "Do not attribute divinity to anything beside Me!"—
and: "Purify My Temple for those who will walk around it,
and those who will stand before it,
and those who will bow down in prostration."
And so, proclaim the pilgrimage to all people:
they will come to you on foot and on every kind of fast conveyance,
coming from every far-away place,
so that they might experience much that shall be of benefit to them,
and that they might glorify God's name.

[22:26-28]

If one honors God's sacred commandments,
it will multiply to your own good in your Sustainer's sight.

[22:30]

---

[48]Temple: The Most Ancient Temple (*Surah* 22:34), which signifies in locality,
the Kaʿbah, and in subtlety, the heart of the human being.

And anyone who honors the symbols set up by God—
truly, these derive their value
from the God-consciousness within the heart.
In that God-consciousness you shall find benefits
until a determined time is fulfilled,
and its goal and end is the Most Ancient Temple.[49]

And always bear in mind your God is the One and Only God:
and so, surrender yourselves to Hu.[50]
And give the glad tiding of God's acceptance to all who are humble—
all those whose hearts tremble with awe whenever God is mentioned,
and all who patiently bear whatever ill befalls them,
and all who are constant in prayer
and spend on others
out of the sustenance We have provided for them.

[22:32-35]

Truly, God will turn aside evil from those who attain to faith;
truly, God does not love the one who betrays his trust
and lacks gratitude.

[22:38]

---

[49]See previous note.
[50]See note 30.

To every community We have appointed ways of worship,
which they ought to observe.
And so, do not let others draw you into arguing about it,
but invite them to your Sustainer:
for you are indeed on the right way.
And if they argue with you, say: "God knows best what you are doing."
Indeed, God will judge between you on the Day of Resurrection
concerning everything about which you would differ.

[22:67-69]

The Faithful

ʾAl-Muʾminūn

Truly, those who live in awe of their Sustainer;
those who have faith in the signs of their Sustainer;
those who do not attribute divinity to any but your Sustainer;
and those who distribute their charity
with their hearts trembling with awe
because they will return to their Sustainer—
it is these who quicken in every good work
and these who are at the forefront.
On no soul do We place a burden greater than it can bear;
with Us is a record which clearly shows the truth:
never will they be wronged.

[23:57-62]

It is He Who has created for you
hearing, sight, feeling, and understanding;
but how seldom are you grateful!
And He has multiplied you through the earth
and to Him you shall be gathered back.
It is He Who gives life and death
and to Him is due the alternation of night and day.
Will you not then understand?

[23:78-80]

83

The Light

'An-Nūr

O you who have attained to faith!
Don't follow Satan's footsteps:
for the one who follows Satan's footsteps, witness,
encourages corruption and all that is contrary to reason.
And were it not for God's blessing with you and His compassion,
not one of you would ever have remained pure,
for it is God who causes whomever He wills to increase in purity:
for God is All-hearing, All-knowing.
And so, do not let those of you who have been graced
with God's favor and ease of circumstance
ever be neglectful of helping their near of kin, and the needy,
and those who have turned from the domain of evil for God's sake,
but let them forgive and endure.
Do you not desire that God should forgive you *your* sins,
seeing that God is Ever Ready to Forgive, and is Most Merciful?

[24:21-22]

Tell the men of faith to lower their gaze
and to be mindful of their chastity:
this will help to increase their purity—
truly, God is aware of all that they do.
And tell the women of faith to lower their gaze
and to be mindful of their chastity,
and not to display their charms beyond what may readily be apparent.

[24:30-31]

God is the Light of the heavens and the earth.
The parable of His light is,
as it were, that of a niche containing a lamp;
the lamp is enclosed in glass, the glass like a radiant star;
lit from a blessed tree—an olive-tree
that is neither of the east nor of the west—
the oil of which would almost give light
even though fire had not touched it: light upon light!
God guides to His light the one who wills to be guided;
and God offers parables to human beings,
since God has full knowledge of all things.

Allāhu nūrus samāwāti wal ʾarḍ.
Mathalu nūrihi kamishkātin fīhā miṣbāḥun, ʾalmiṣbāḥu
fī zujājatin, ʾazzujājatu kaʾannahā
kawkabun durriyyun yūqadu min shajaratim mubārakatin
zaytūnatil lā sharqiyyatin wa lā gharbiyyatin
yakādu zaytuhā yuḍeeʾu
wa law lam tamsas-hu naar.
Nūrun ʿalā nuur.
Yahdillāhu linūrihi man yashaaʾ.
Wa yaḍribullāhul amthāla linnaas.
Wallāhu bikulli shayʾin ʿaleem.

[24:35]

85

In the houses which God has allowed to be raised
so that His/Her name shall be remembered in them,
there are those who praise His/Her limitless glory
morning and evening—
those whom neither business nor striving after gain
can turn from the remembrance of God,
and from constancy in prayer, and from charity:
who are filled with awe
of the Day on which all hearts and eyes will be transformed,
who only hope that God will give them recompense
in accordance with the best of their actions,
and give them even more out of His/Her blessing:

for God grants sustenance to whom He/She wills, beyond all reckoning.

Wallāhu yarzuqu man yashaa'u bighayri ḥisaab.

[24:36-38]

Are you not aware that it is God whose limitless glory
all creatures in the heavens and on earth praise,
even the birds as they outspread their wings?
Indeed, each of them knows how to pray to Him and glorify Him;
and God has full knowledge of all that they do:
for God's is the sovereignty of the heavens and the earth,
and with God is all journeys' end.

[24:41-42]

Are you not aware that it is God Who causes the clouds to move,
then joins them, and piles them up,
until you see rain come forth from among them?
And He it is Who sends down from the skies, bit by bit,
mountainous masses of clouds charged with hail,
striking whomever He wills,
and turning it away from whomever He wills,
while the flash of His lightning is almost blinding!
It is God Who causes the cycling of night and day:
in this, witness, surely there is a lesson for all who have eyes to see!
And it is God Who has created all animals out of water,
and He has willed that among them
are some that crawl on their bellies,
and some that walk on two legs,
and some that walk on four.
God creates what He wills:
for, truly, God has the power to will anything.
Indeed, from on high
We have bestowed messages clearly showing the truth;
but God guides to a straight way only the one who wills to be guided.

[24: 43-46]

The Criterion

'Al-Furqān

Blessed is the One Who sent down the Criterion to His servant
that it might be a counsel to all the world.

[25:1]

Say: "The Qur'ān was sent down
by the One Who knows all the Mysteries
of the heavens and the earth:
truly, that One is Ever-Forgiving, Most Merciful."

[25:6]

And the messengers whom We sent before you were all human beings
who ate food and walked through the streets;
We have made some of you as a test for others.
Will you have patience?
For God is One Who sees.

[25:20]

Those who reject faith say:
"Why is the Qurʾān not revealed to him all at once?"
It is so that by this We may strengthen your heart;
and We have related it to you in well-arranged stages,
little by little.

[25:32]

Have you not turned your vision towards your Sustainer?
See how He lengthens the shadow!
If He willed He could make it stand still!
But We have made the sun its guide,
and then We draw it in towards Ourselves—a contraction by easy stages.
And He it is Who makes the night as a robe for you,
and sleep as repose, and makes every day a resurrection.
And He it is Who sends the winds as heralds of glad tidings
preceding His Mercy.
And We send down purifying water from the sky
that with it We may give life to a dead land
and assuage the thirst of things We have created—
cattle and people in great numbers.
And We have distributed it among them
so that they may celebrate Our praises—
but most people are reluctant to be anything but ungrateful.

[25:45-50]

It is God Who has given freedom to the two bodies of flowing water:
one palatable and sweet and the other salty and bitter;
yet He/She has made a barrier between them,
a threshold which they cannot cross.
It is He/She Who has created the human being from water
and endowed relationships of lineage and marriage:
for your Sustainer's power extends over all things.

[25:53-54]

But We only sent you to give glad news and counsel.
Say: "No reward do I ask of you for it but this: that each one who will
may take a straight path to his Lord."
And put your trust in the One Who lives and does not die;
and celebrate His praise;
and well-aware is He of the shortcomings of His servants—
He Who created the heavens and the earth
and all that is between in six days
and is firmly settled on the Throne of power,
God, the Infinitely Compassionate One:
ask then about Him of one who is aware.

[25:56-59]

Blessed is He/She Who made constellations in the skies
and placed there a lamp and a moon giving light;
And it is He/She Who made the night and the day to follow each other,
for such as have the will to celebrate His/Her praises
or to show their gratitude.
And the servants of the Infinitely Compassionate One
are those who walk on the earth in humility
and when the ignorant address them they say, "Peace!"—
those who spend the night in adoration of their Sustainer
in prostration and standing straight.

[25:61-64]

And whoever repents and does good
has truly turned to God by repentance.
Those who never bear witness to that which is false
and if they encounter frivolity pass by it with honor;
those who when they are counseled with the signs of their Sustainer
don't act as if they were deaf or blind;
and those who pray, "O our Sustainer!
grant us spouses and offspring who will be the comfort of our eyes
and give us the grace to lead the righteous."—
those are the ones who will be rewarded
with the highest place in heaven because of their patient perseverance;
there they shall be met with greetings and peace,
dwelling there—what a beautiful abode and place of rest!

[25:71-76]

The Poets

'Ash-Shu'arā'

The Sustainer and Cherisher of the Worlds,
Who created me, it is He Who guides me,
Who gives me food and drink
and when I am ill it is He Who restores me to health,
Who will cause me to die and then to live,
and Who I hope will forgive me my faults on the Day of Reckoning.
O my Sustainer! bestow wisdom on me and join me with the righteous;
grant me the ability to convey the truth to those who will come after me;
make me one of the inheritors of the Garden of Bliss;
forgive my father for being among those astray;
and let me not be in disgrace on the Day when we will be raised up,
the Day when neither wealth nor children will be of use,
but only the one who brings to God a sound heart.

(Prayer of Abraham)

[26:77-89]

So do not call on any other god with God
or you will be among those under reproach.
And counsel your nearest kinsfolk,
and lower the wings of your tenderness
toward the faithful who follow you.

[26:213-215]

The Ants

ʾAn-Naml

So he smiled, amused at her speech,[51]
and he said:

"O my Sustainer!
so direct me that I may be grateful
for Your blessings which You have bestowed on me and on my parents
and that I may do the good work that will please You;
and admit me by Your Grace
among the ranks of Your righteous servants."

(Prayer of Solomon)

Rabbi ʾawziʿnee ʾan ʾashkura
niʿmatakal latee ʾanʿamta ʿalayya wa ʿalā wālidayya
wa ʾan ʾaʿmala ṣāliḥan tarḍāhu
wa ʾadkhilnī biraḥmatika
fī ʿibādikaṣ ṣāliḥeen.

[27:19]

---

[51] This prayer of Solomon is in response to the words of an ant. As his ranks were approaching, she called out to her community, "O you ants! Go back into your dwellings that Solomon and his hosts might not crush you unawares." [27:15] Solomon offers his prayer in gratitude for his comprehension, and the compassion and admiration for all of nature which God had bestowed upon him.

93

Who listens to the distressed soul when it calls on Him
and who relieves its suffering and makes you inheritors of the earth?
Can there be another god besides God?
How little you pay attention!
Or who guides you through the depths of darkness on land and sea
and who sends the winds as heralds of glad news preceding His mercy?
Can there be another god besides God?
Exalted is God beyond what they associate with Him!
Or who originates creation, then renews it,
and who gives you sustenance from heaven and earth?
Can there be another god besides God?
Say: "Present your argument if you speak the truth!"
Say: "None in the heavens or on earth
except God knows what is hidden."
Nor can they perceive when they shall be raised from the dead.

[27:62-65]

Say: "As for me, I have been commanded to serve the Sustainer of this City,[52]
the One Who has sanctified it and to Whom all things belong;
and I am commanded
to be of those who bow in surrender to God's Will
and to recite the Qurʾān."
And if any accept guidance they do so for the good of their own souls
and if any stray, say: "I am only a warner."
And say: "Praise be to God Who will soon show you His signs
so that you shall know them."—
and your Sustainer is not unmindful of anything that you do.

[27:91-93]

---

[52]I.e., Mecca, where the first temple devoted to the One God was built originally by Abraham. "City" here may also have the meaning of "the whole human being"— body, mind, and heart.

The Story

ʾAl-Qaṣaṣ

So We sent this inspiration to the mother of Moses:
"Nurse, but when you fear for him cast him into the river,
and do not be afraid or grieve: for We shall restore him to you,
and We shall make him one of Our messengers."
Then Pharaoh's people caught him up:
it was intended that he should be an adversary
and a cause of sorrow to them,
for Pharaoh and Haman and their hosts were erring people.
Pharaoh's wife said: "Here is a joy of the eye for me and for you:
do not slay him. It may be that he will be of use to us,
or we may adopt him as a son."
And they did not perceive what was happening!
But an emptiness came to the heart of Moses' mother:
she was about to disclose him had We not strengthened her heart
so that she might remain one of faith.
And she said to his sister, "Follow him."
So his sister watched him in the guise of a stranger,
and they did not know.
And We ordained that at first he should refuse to nurse
until she said: "Shall I point out to you
the people of a house that will nourish and raise him for you
and be sincerely devoted to him?"
And so We restored him to his mother that her eye might be comforted,
that she might not grieve,
and that she might know that the promise of God is true;
but most of them do not understand.

[28:7-13]

95

Now when Moses had fulfilled the appointed time
and was traveling with his family,
he perceived a fire in the direction of Mount Ṭūr.[53]
He said to his family: "Wait; I perceive a fire;
I hope to bring you from there some news
or a burning torch that you may warm yourselves."
But when he came to it a voice was heard
from the right bank of the valley from a tree in sacred ground:
"O Moses! Truly, I am God, the Lord of the Worlds. . . .
Now throw your rod!"
But when he saw it moving as though it were a snake,
he turned back in retreat and did not retrace his steps:
"O Moses! draw near and do not be afraid:
for you are of those who are secure."

[28:29-31]

Twice will they be given their reward
because they have persevered: they have turned aside evil with good,
and they give to others from what We have given to them.
And when they hear vain talk they turn away from it and say:
"To us our deeds and to you yours;
peace be with you: we do not seek the ignorant."

[28:54-55]

---

[53]Mount Ṭūr: Mt. Sinai

And your Sustainer knows all that their hearts conceal
and all that they reveal.
And He is God: there is no god but He.
To him be praise at the first and at the last:
for Him is the Command, and to Him shall you return.
Say: "Do you see? If God were to make the night perpetual over you
until the Day of Reckoning, what god is there other than God
who can give you enlightenment?
Will you not then pay attention?"
Say: "Do you see? If God were to make the Day perpetual over you
until the Day of Reckoning, what god is there other than God
who can give you a night in which you can rest?
Then will you not see?"
It is out of His Mercy that He has made for you night and day—
that you may rest within it, and that you may seek His Grace,
and so that you might be grateful.

[28:69-73]

Qarun was doubtless among the people of Moses;
but he acted insolently towards them:
such were the treasures We had bestowed on him
that their very keys would have been a burden
to a body of strong men.
Witness, his people said to him: "Don't gloat,
for God does not love those who take pride in riches.
But with that which God has bestowed on you
seek the Home of the Hereafter,
yet do not forget your portion in this world—
do good as God has been good to you
and do not seek to do harm in the land:
for God does not love those who act harmfully."

[28:76-77]

If anyone does good, the reward to him is better than his deed;
but if anyone does harm,
those who do harm are only punished to the extent
of that which they have done.

[28:84]

And you had not expected that the Book would be sent to you
except as a Mercy from your Sustainer;
so do not lend support in any way to the deniers.
And let nothing inhibit you from the signs of God
after they have been revealed to you;
and invite to your Sustainer,
and do not be among those who join gods with God.
And do not call on another god besides God.

There is no god but He.
Everything is perishing except His Face.
To Him belongs the Command,
and to Him will you all return.

Laa 'ilāha 'illā Hū.
Kullu shay'in hālikun 'illā wajhah.
Lahul ḥukmu
wa 'ilayhi turja'uun.

[28:86–88]

The Spider

'Al-'Ankabūt

Say: "Travel through the earth
and see how God originated creation.
Even so will God create again,
for God has power over all things."

[29:20]

The parable of those who take protectors other than God
is that of the Spider who builds itself a house;
but truly, the Spider's house is the flimsiest of houses if they only knew.
Truly, your Sustainer knows what they call upon besides Him/Her
and He/She is Most Exalted, the All-Wise.
And such are the parables We offer humankind
but only those of inner knowing understand them.
In true proportions God created the heavens and the earth:
truly, in that is a sign for those who have faith.

[29:41-44]

Recite what is sent of the Book by inspiration to you
and establish regular prayer:
for prayer restrains from shameful and unjust deeds,
and remembrance of God is surely the greatest of all things in life.
And God knows that which you do.

[29:45]

O my servants who have faith!
truly, My earth is spacious,
so serve Me alone!
Every soul shall have a taste of death:
in the end to Us shall you all be brought back.
But those who have faith and do good deeds,
to them shall We give a home in the Garden—
lofty mansions beneath which rivers flow—
to dwell there always,
an excellent reward for those who act rightly—
those who persevere in patience
and put their trust in their Sustainer.

[29:56-59]

How many are the creatures that do not carry their own sustenance?
It is God Who feeds them and you:
for He/She is the One Who Hears and the One Who Knows.

[29:60]

And those strive in Our cause—
We will certainly guide them to Our Paths:
For, truly, God is with those who do right.

[29:69]

The Byzantines

ʾAr-Rūm

The promise of God—
never does God deviate from His promise;
but most people do not understand.
They know only the external in the life of this world;
don't they ever reflect within their own minds?
Only for just ends and for a determined time
did God create the heavens and the earth and all between them:
yet there are truly many among humankind
who deny the meeting with their Sustainer!
Do they not travel through the earth
and see what was the end of those before them?
They were superior to them in strength; they tilled the soil
and populated it more extensively than these have done;
there came to them their messengers with clear signs.
It was not God Who wronged them
but they who wronged their own souls.

[30:6-9]

So glorify God when you reach the evening
and when you rise in the morning;
for all praise belongs to Him in the heavens and on earth,
and also in the late afternoon and when the day passes its zenith.
It is He Who brings out the living from the dead
and Who brings out the dead from the living,
and Who gives life to the earth after it has died,
and even so shall you all be brought forth.

[30:17-19]

Among the signs of God is this: that He created you from dust,
and then, see how you become human beings ranging far and wide!
And among His Signs is this: that He created for you mates
from among yourselves that you may dwell in tranquillity with them,
and He engenders love and compassion between you;
truly in that are signs for those who reflect.
And among His signs is the creation of the heavens and the earth
and the variations in your languages and your colors:
truly in that are signs for those who know.

And among His signs is your sleep by night and by day
as well as your quest for provision from His Bounty:
truly, in that are signs for those who pay attention.
And among His Signs He shows you the lightning
by way both of fear and of hope
and He sends down rain from the sky
and with it gives life to the earth after it is dead:
truly, in that are signs for those who are wise.

And among His signs is this:
that heaven and earth stand by His Command.
Then, when He calls you from the earth by a single call,
witness, you will emerge.
To Him belongs every being that is in the heavens and on earth:
all devoutly obey Him.
It is He Who begins the unfolding of creation,
then repeats it; and it is most easy for Him.
For His is the essence of all that is most sublime
in the heavens and the earth:
for He is Exalted in Might, All-Wise.

[30:20-27]

So set your face steadily and truly to the faith,
turning away from all that is false
according to the pattern with which He has made humankind;
do not allow to be corrupted that which God has made.
That is the true way,
but most people do not understand.
Turn in repentance to Him and remain conscious of Him:
be constant in prayer
and do not be among those who join gods with God,
those who split apart their religion
and become sects—each group celebrating alone that which is with itself!

[30:30-32]

So give what is due to those related to you,
to the needy, and to the one who is journeying.
That is best for those who seek the Countenance of God
and it is they who will prosper.

[30:38-39]

Among His signs is this: that He sends the winds
as heralds of joyous news giving you a taste of His mercy,
that the ships may sail by His command,
and that you may seek of His abundance: so that you might be grateful.
We did indeed send before you messengers to their peoples
and they came to them with clear signs;
then, to those who went beyond bounds, We apportioned retribution,
for it was Our obligation to help those who had faith.
It is God Who sends the winds, and they raise the clouds;
then He spreads them in the sky as He wills
and breaks them into fragments
until you see rain-drops flow forth;
then, when He has made them reach those of His servants that He wills,
see how they rejoice!

[30:46-48]

So patiently persevere: for truly God's promise is true;
and do not let those who have no certainty of faith
shake your certainty.

[30:60]

Luqmān

We bestowed this wisdom on Luqman:
"Be grateful to God."
Anyone who is grateful does so to the profit of his own soul;
but if anyone is ungrateful, truly God is free of all needs,
and ever to be praised.

[31:12]

Witness, Luqman counseled his son:
"O my dear son! Do not ascribe divine power to any beside God:
for such false worship is indeed a profound wrong-doing."

And We have enjoined upon the human being
goodness towards his parents;
in travail upon travail did his mother bear him
and in two years was his weaning.
Be grateful to Me and to your parents:
with Me is all journey's end.
But if they strive to make you ascribe divinity, side by side with Me,
to something which is contrary to your knowing,
do not obey them;
yet bear them company in this life with kindness,
and follow the way of those who turn to Me:
in the end you will all return to Me
and I will make clear to you the truth of all that you were doing.

[31:13-15]

"O my dear son!" continued Luqman,
"If there were anything the weight of even a mustard-seed,
and it were within a rock or in the heavens or on earth,
God will bring it to light:
for God comprehends the subtlest mysteries and is All-Aware.
O my dear son! Be constant in prayer,
encourage what is just, and forbid what is wrong,
and bear with patient perseverance whatever comes to you;
witness, this is something upon which to set one's heart.
And do not turn away from people with pride
nor walk in insolence on the earth;
for God does not love the arrogant boaster.
And be modest in your bearing and lower your voice;
for without a doubt, the harshest of sounds is the braying of the ass."

[31:16-19]

Don't you see that God has made in service to you
all that is in the heavens and on earth
and has made His bounties flow to you
in abundant measure, seen and unseen?
Yet still there are among humankind those who dispute about God—
those without knowledge, and without guidance,
and without any light-giving revelation!

[31:20]

Whoever submits his or her whole self to God and is a doer of good
has indeed grasped the most trustworthy hand-hold:
for with God rests the final outcome of all endeavors.

*Wa man yuslim wajhahuu 'ilallāhi wa huwa muḥsinun
faqadis tamsaka bil ʿurwatil wuthqaa.
Wa 'ilallāhi ʿāqibatul 'umuur.*

[31:22]

And if all the trees on earth were pens and the Ocean were ink
with seven Oceans behind it to supplement it
still, the Words of God would not be exhausted:
for God is Exalted in Power, All-Wise.

[31:27]

And your creation or your resurrection
is in no other way than as a single soul:
for God is He Who Hears and Sees all things.

[31:28]

Truly, the knowledge of the Last Hour is with God alone.
It is He Who sends down rain
and He Who knows what is within the wombs.
Nor does anyone know what it is that he will earn the coming day;
nor does anyone know in what land he is to die.
Truly, with God is complete knowledge
and He is All-Aware.

[31:34]

Prostration

ʾAs-Sajdah

Only those have faith in Our signs
who when they are recited to them
fall down, and prostrating themselves in adoration
celebrate the praises of their Lord,
nor are they ever bloated with pride.
They are moved to rise from their beds of sleep
while they call on their Sustainer in awe and in hope;
and they spend on others out of the sustenance
which We have bestowed on them.
Now no person knows what delights of the eye
are kept hidden for them as a reward for their deeds.
Is the one who has faith no better than the one who is corrupt?
They are not equal.
For those who have faith and do righteous deeds
are Gardens as welcoming homes for that which they have done.

[32:15-19]

The Allies

ʾAl-Aḥzāb

O Prophet!
Stand in awe of God and do not pay attention
to the deniers and the hypocrites:
truly, God is All-Knowing and Truly Wise.
But follow that which comes to you by inspiration from your Sustainer:
for God is Well-Aware of all that you do.
And put your trust in God, for God suffices as your Guardian of Affairs.

[33:1-3]

Truly, in the Messenger of God
you have a beautiful standard
for anyone whose hope is in God and the Last Day
and who remembers God unceasingly.

[33:21]

110

For men and women who surrender themselves to God,
for men and women of faith,
for devout men and women, for true men and women,
for men and women who are patient and persevering,
for men and women who humble themselves before God,
for men and women who give in charity,
for men and women who fast,
for men and women who guard their chastity,
and for men and women who remember God unceasingly,
for them has God readied forgiveness and a supreme recompense.

[33:35]

O you who have faith!
celebrate God's praises, and do this often;
and glorify Him morning and evening.
He it is Who sends blessings on you as do His angels
that He may bring you out of the depths of Darkness into the Light:
and He is Full of Mercy to the faithful.
Their greeting on the Day they meet Him will be "Peace!"
And He has readied for them a most generous recompense.

[33:41-44]

God and His angels send blessings on the Prophet:
O you who have faith, bless him
and greet him with complete respect.

[33:56]

O you who have faith! Stand in awe of God
and always speak a word on behalf of that which is right and true:
that He may make your behavior whole and sound
and forgive you your mistakes.
The one who heeds God and His Messenger
has already attained a mighty success.
Truly, We offered the Trust
to the heavens, and to the earth, and to the mountains;
but they refused to undertake it, as they were afraid of it—
but the human being undertook it
though he was indeed unjust and foolish,
so that God must chastise the hypocrites, men and women,
and the deniers, men and women,
yet God turns in mercy to the faithful, men and women:
for God is Ever-ready to Forgive, Infinitely Merciful.

[33:70-73]

Sheba

Saba'

And We bestowed Our grace upon David:
"O you Mountains! Sing with him the praises of God!
And you birds!"
And We softened all sharpness in him,
and inspired him: "Make protective garments,
balancing well the links of the chain,
and do good deeds unceasingly;
for be sure, I see all that you do."

[34:10-11]

Say: "Truly my Sustainer grants abundant sustenance
or bestows it in meager measure
to such of His servants as He wills;
and whatever you spend on others, He replaces it:
for He is the Best of Providers."

[34:39]

Say: "I counsel you one thing only:
be ever conscious of standing before God—
whether you are in the company of others or alone
and reflect: your companion is not possessed:
he is only a warner to you of an intense suffering to come."
Say: "No reward do I ask of you; it is in your own interest.
My reward is with God alone, and to all things He/She is Witness."
Say: "Truly my Sustainer hurls the Truth—
He/She Who has complete knowledge of that which is hidden."
Say: "The Truth has arrived,
and falsehood can create nothing new, nor can it revive."
Say: "If I go astray I only stray to the hurt of my own soul;
but if I am on the right path,
it is because of inspiration to me from my Sustainer—
it is He/She Who Hears all things; He/She Who is always near."

[34:46–50]

The Originator

Al-Fāṭir

Praise be to God
Who originally created the heavens and the earth;
Who made the angels messengers with wings—
two or three or four;
Hu[54] adds to creation as Hu pleases: for God has power over all things.
What God out of His mercy bestows on humankind,
none can withhold;
what He withholds, none can grant separately from Him,
for He is the Exalted in Power, the All-Wise.
O people! Call to mind God's grace to you!
Is there a creator other than God to give you sustenance
from heaven or from earth?
There is no god but He:
how then are you so misled from the Truth?

[35:1-3]

---

[54] See note 30.

Nor can one who bears burdens bear the burden of another.
If one weighed down by his load should call another to help him carry it
not the least portion of it could be carried
even if he is one's close relation.
You can counsel only those who stand in awe of their Sustainer,
though He is unseen,
and are constant in prayer,
and whoever purifies himself/herself
does so for the benefit of his/her own soul;
and all are journeying to God.
The blind and the seeing are not alike,
nor are the depths of darkness and the light,
nor are the shade and the heat of the sun;
nor are alike those that are living and those that are dead.
God can make any that He/She wills to hear;
but you cannot make those hear who are buried in graves.
You are nothing but a warner.
Truly, We have sent you with truth as a bearer of joyous news
and as a warner;
and never has there been a people
without a warner having lived among them.

[35:18-24]

Do you not see that God sends down rain from the sky?
With it We then produce fruits of many colors.
And in the mountains are areas
that are white, and red of various shades, and black intense in hue.
Even so among people and crawling creatures and cattle
are those of various colors.
Those among His Servants who have knowledge stand in awe of God:
for God is Almighty, Often-Forgiving.
Those who recite the Book of God and are constant in prayer,
and distribute out of what We have provided for them,
secretly and openly, hope for an exchange that will never fail:
for He will pay them their due,
no, He will give them even more out of His abundance;
for He is Often-Forgiving, Always Responsive to Gratitude.

[35:27-30]

Truly, God knows all the hidden things
of the heavens and the earth:
truly, He has complete knowledge of all that is within hearts.

[35:38]

O Thou Human Being

Yā-Sīn

Then there came running from the farthest part of the City
a man saying, "O my people! follow these message-bearers,
follow those who ask no reward of you
and are themselves rightly guided.
It would not be reasonable of me if I did not serve
the One Who created me
and to Whom you shall all be brought back.
Shall I take other gods besides God?
If the Most Gracious should intend some adversity for me,
of no use whatever will their intercession be for me
nor can they deliver me.
If I were to do so, I would indeed, obviously be in error.
As for me I have faith in the Sustainer of you all: listen, then, to me!"
It was said: "Enter thou the Garden."
He said, "Ah me! would that my People knew what I know!"

[36:20–26]

A Sign for them is the earth that is dead;
We give it life and produce grain from it
of which you eat.
And We produce there orchards with date-palms and vines
and We cause springs to gush forth from within it,
that they may enjoy the fruits there.
It was not their hands that made this;
will they not then give thanks?

Limitless in His glory is God Who created in pairs
all things that the earth produces
as well as their own humankind
as well as things of which they have no knowledge.
And a sign for them is the night:
We withdraw the day from it and see how they are plunged in darkness;
And the Sun runs his course for a period designated for him
that is determined by the will of the Almighty, the All-Knowing.
And the moon—We have measured mansions for her to pass through
until curved like a withered date-stalk she returns.
The sun is not permitted to overtake the moon
nor can the night go beyond the day,
but each moves easily in its lawful way.

[36:33-40]

Then on that Day not a soul will be wronged in the least
and you shall be recompensed only for that which you have done.
Truly the companions of the Garden
shall that Day be wholly immersed in joy;
they and their companions will rest on couches in shady groves;
fruits will be there for them,
and theirs shall be whatever they could ask for;

"Peace!"—the Word of a Most Merciful Sustainer!

Salām qawlam mir Rabbir Raḥeem.

[36:54-58]

We have not instructed the Prophet in poetry
nor is it appropriate for him: this is no less than a Message
and a Qurʾān making things clear:
that it may give counsel to any who are living
and that the Word may stand forth
against the deniers of Truth.

[36:69-70]

Does man not see that it is We Who created Him from sperm?
Yet witness! He stands in open opposition!
And he makes likenesses for us and forgets his own creation:
he says, "Who can give life to decomposed bones?"
Say: "He will give them life Who created them in the beginning!
For He is supremely skilled in every kind of creation!
The same Who produces for you fire out of the green tree;
witness, how you kindle your own fires from it!
Is not He Who created the heavens and the earth
able to create their like?"
Of course! For He is the Creator Supreme in skill and knowledge!

Truly, when He intends a thing, His command is "Be" and it is!
So glory to Him in Whose hands is the dominion of all things;
and to Him will you all return.

*Innamaa 'amruhuu 'izhaa 'arāda shay'an
'an yaqūla lahu "Kun" fayakuun.
Fa subḥānal lazhī biyadihī malakūtu kulli shay'in
wa 'ilayhi turja'uun.*

[36:77-83]

Those Ranged in Ranks

ʾAṣ-Ṣāffāt

By those who range themselves in ranks
and so are strong in repelling evil,
and so proclaim the message!
Truly, truly, your God is One!
The Sustainer of the heavens and of the earth
and all that is between them, and Lord of every point of sunrise!

[37:1-5]

The sincere servants of God,
for them is an appointed nourishment—
fruits, and honor, and dignity,
in gardens of felicity,
facing each other on thrones of happiness:
a cup will be passed around from a clear-flowing fountain,
crystal-clear and delightful to those who drink of it.

[37:40-46]

Limitless in His glory is your Sustainer, the Lord of Almightiness—
beyond anything by which they may try to define Him!
And peace be with all the Messengers!
And all praise belongs to God alone, the Sustainer of all the Worlds.

[37:180-182]

Ṣād[55]

Bear with patience what they say
and remember Our servant David,
he who was endowed with inner strength: for he always turned to Us.
It was We Who made the hills declare Our praises in unison with him
at nightfall and at break of day.
And the birds gathered: all with him did turn.
We strengthened his dominion
and gave him wisdom and sound judgment in speech and decisions.

[38:17-20]

O David! We did indeed make you a representative on earth.
So judge between people with truth,
and do not follow your lusts, for they will mislead you from God's path:
those who wander from God's path meet a sorrowful chastisement,
for they are forgetting the Day of Reckoning.

[38:26]

This Book of blessings We have sent down to you—
so that they may meditate on its signs[56]
and that people of insight might take them to heart.

[38:29]

---

[55]See note 40.
[56]sign: *ayats*=verses as well as "significations"

To David We gave Solomon, what an excellent servant!
He always turned to Us!
See how there were brought before him at nightfall
chargers of the highest breeding, and swift of foot.
And he said, "Truly, I love the love of the Good
because of remembrance of my Sustainer."

[38:30-32]

And remember Our servants Abraham, Isaac, and Jacob,
endowed with inner strength and vision.
Truly, We purified them
by means of the remembrance of the Life to Come.
They were in Our sight, truly, among the elect and the Good.
And remember Ishmail, Elisha, and Zul-Kifl:
each of them was among the companions of the Good.
This is a reminder:
and truly, awaiting the God-conscious is a beautiful place of return.

[38:45-49]

Say:[57] "No reward do I ask of you for this,
nor am I of those who pretend to be what they are not.
This is no less than a reminder to all the worlds.
And after a while you shall certainly know the truth of it."

[38:86-88]

---

[57] God instructs Muhammad regarding his role as messenger.

The Throngs

ʾAz-Zumar

Is one who worships devoutly during the hours of the night,
prostrating himself or standing,
who keeps in awareness the Hereafter,
and who places his hope in the Mercy of his Sustainer
like one who does not?
Say: "Are those equal, those who know and those who do not know?
It is those who are endowed with insight who receive counsel."
Say: "O you My servants who have come to faith!
Be conscious of your Sustainer:
good is for those who persevere in doing good in this world.
Spacious is God's earth!
Those who patiently persevere
will truly receive a reward beyond measure!"

[39:9-10]

Say: "It is God I serve with my sincere devotion."

[39:14]

But it is for those who remain conscious of their Sustainer
that lofty mansions one above another have been built.
Through them flow rivers—God's promise;
never does God fail in His promise.
Don't you see that God sends down rain from the sky
and leads it through springs in the earth?
Then with it He causes growth of varied colors to emerge,
then it withers; you will see it turn yellow;
then He makes it shrivel and crumble to dust.
Truly in this is a Message of remembrance for people of insight.
Is one whose heart God has opened to surrender
so that he is illumined by a light from his Sustainer
no better than one who is hard-hearted?
Woe to those whose hearts are hardened
against remembrance of God!
They obviously wander astray!
God has revealed the most beautiful message in the form of a Book
consistent within itself, repeating its teaching in various guises—
the skins of those who stand in awe of their Lord tremble with it;
then their skins and their hearts soften
with the remembrance of God.
Such is God's guidance:
with it He guides the one who wills to be guided,
but those whom God lets stray have none to guide them.

[39:20-23]

God offers a parable:
a person belonging to many partners at variance with each other
and a person belonging entirely to one master:
are those two equal in state?
All praise belongs to God! But most of them do not comprehend.

[39:29]

And the one who brings the Truth and the one who stands with it,
it is they, they who do right.
They shall have all that they yearn for in the presence of their Sustainer,
such is the reward of those who do good,
so that God will divert from them the worst in their deeds
and give them their recompense
according to the best of that which they have done.

[39:33-35]

Say: "O my Servants who have transgressed against your own selves!
Do not despair of Allah's Compassion:
for Allah forgives all mistakes:
for He/She is Often-Forgiving, Infinitely Merciful.
Turn to your Sustainer and surrender to Him/Her
before the suffering comes upon you: after that you will not be helped.
And before the penalty suddenly comes upon you
without your perceiving it,
follow the best of that which your Sustainer has revealed to you!"

[39:53-55]

And those who remain conscious of their Sustainer
will be led to the Garden in throngs:
until witness, they arrive there: its gates will be opened,
and its keepers will say, "Peace be with you! You have done well!
Enter here to dwell."
They will say, "Praise be to God
Who has truly fulfilled His promise to us
and has bestowed on us this expanse as our inheritance;
we can dwell in the Garden as we will.
What an excellent recompense for those who labor rightly!"
And you will see the angels surrounding the throne of authority
singing glory and praises to their Lord.
The judgement between them all will be in justice.
And it will be said, "All praise is due to God,
the Sustainer of all the Worlds!"

[39:73-75]

Forgiving

Ghāfir

Those who sustain the throne of authority and those around it
sing glory and praises to their Sustainer,
have faith in Him/Her, and ask forgiveness for those who have faith:
"Our Sustainer!
You embrace all things within Your compassion and knowledge.
Forgive then those who turn in repentance and follow Your Path,
and preserve them from suffering through the blazing fire!
And O our Sustainer! Bring them into the Gardens of Eternity
which You have promised to them and to the righteous
among their parents, their spouses, and their descendents!
For You are Almighty, Truly Wise.
And preserve them from harmful deeds;
and any whom You preserve from harmful deeds,
on that Day, truly, You will have graced with Your Mercy.
And that will be the ultimate success."

[40:7-9]

The one who had faith said further: "O my People!
follow me: I will lead you to the right path.
O my people! This present life is just a brief convenience;
it is the Hereafter that is the enduring Home.
The one who does evil will only be requited with its like;
and anyone who does that which is good, whether man or woman,
and who has faith, these will enter the Garden—
there they will have infinite abundance."

[40:38-40]

Earlier, We gave Moses guidance,
and We gave the Book as an inheritance to the children of Israel—
a guide and a reminder to people of insight.
So patiently persevere, for God's promise is true;
and ask forgiveness for your mistakes
and celebrate the praises of your Sustainer
in the evening and in the morning.

[40:53-55]

And your Sustainer says: "Call on Me; I will answer you."

Wa qāla rabbukumud-d'ūnee 'astajib lakum.

[40:60]

It is God Who has made the night for you that you may rest in it
and the day as that which helps you to see.
Truly, God is limitless in His abundant grace to humankind,
yet most people are ungrateful.
Such is God, your Sustainer, the Creator of all things—
there is no god but He.
Then, how can you be so deluded about the Truth!

[40:61-62]

130

It is God Who has made for you the earth as a resting place
and the sky as a canopy
and has given you shapes and made your shapes beautiful
and has provided for you sustenance of pure and good things—
such is God, your Sustainer.

So Glory to God, the Sustainer of all the Worlds!
He is the Ever-Living: there is no god but He.
Call upon Him, offering Him sincere devotion.
Praise be to God, Sustainer of all the Worlds!

[40:64-65]

Clearly Spelled-Out

Fuṣṣilat

He is the Sustainer of the Worlds.
He established the mountains standing high above it
and bestowed blessings on the earth,
and measured all things there to give them nourishment
in due proportion,
in four aeons in accordance with the needs of those who seek.
And He comprehended in His design the sky which had been as smoke.
He said to it and to the earth: "Come together willingly or unwillingly."
They said: "We come in willing obedience."
So He completed them as seven heavens in two aeons
and He assigned to each heaven its duty and command.
And We adorned the lower heaven with lights
and provided it with protection.
Such is the Command of the Almighty, the All-Knowing.

[41:9-12]

In the case of those who say "Our Sustainer is God"
and further stand straight and steadfast,
the angels come down to them: "Do not be fearful, and do not grieve!
But receive the glad news of the Garden which you were promised!
We are your protectors in this life and in the Hereafter.
There you shall have all that for which your souls long;
there you shall have all that you ask for!
A welcoming gift from One Often-Forgiving, Most Merciful!"

[41:30-32]

Among His Signs are the night and the day and the sun and moon.
Do not adore the sun and the moon but adore God
Who created them, if it is Him you wish to serve.
But if some are arrogant, it doesn't matter:
for in the presence of your Lord
are those who celebrate His praises by night and by day.
And they never tire.
And among His Signs is this: you see the earth barren and desolate;
but when We send down rain to it, it is stirred to life and yields increase.
Truly, He Who gives life to the earth
can surely give life to those who are dead.
For He has power over all things.

[41:37-39]

We will show them Our signs on the farthest horizons
and within their own selves
until it becomes manifest to them that this is the Truth.
Is it not enough that your Lord is witness to all things?
Indeed! Are they in doubt concerning the Meeting with their Lord?
Ah, truly! it is He Who encompasses all things!

Sanurīhim ʾayātinā fil ʾafāqi
wa fee ʾanfusihim
ḥattā yatabayyana lahum ʾannahul ḥaqq.
ʾAwalam yakfi birabbika ʾannahu ʿalā kulli shayʾin shaheed.
ʾAlaa ʾinnahum fī miryatim mil liqaaʾi rabbihim.
ʾAlaa ʾinnahu bikulli shayʾim muḥeeṭ.

[41:53-54]

133

Consultation

ʾAsh-Shūrā

Whatever it is in which you differ
the decision of it rests with God.
Such is God my Sustainer:
in Him I trust and to Him do I always turn.

*Wa makhtalaftum fīhi min shayʾin
faḥukmuhuu ʾilallaah.
Zhālikumullāhu Rabbī
ʿalayhi tawakkaltu wa ʾilayhi ʾuneeb.*

[42:10]

The Originator of the heavens and the earth—
He has made for you pairs from among yourselves
and pairs among cattle:
by this means He multiplies you; there is nothing whatever like Him
and He is the All-hearing, the All-Seeing.
To Him belong the keys of the heavens and the earth;
He grants abundant sustenance
or bestows it in meager measure to whom He wills:
for He knows well all things.
The same clear Path has He established for you
as that which He enjoined on Noah,
that which We have sent by inspiration to you,
and that which We designated for Abraham, Moses, and Jesus:
that you should steadfastly uphold the Faith
and make no divisions within it.
To those who worship other things than God,
the way to which you call them may appear difficult.
God draws to Himself those who are willing
and guides to Himself everyone who turns to Him.

[42:11-13]

And so, call out to them
and stand steadfast as you have been commanded,
and do not follow their likes and dislikes, but say:
"I have faith in the Book which God has bestowed from on high;
and I am asked to judge justly between you.
God is our Sustainer and your Sustainer.
To us belongs the responsibility for our deeds, and to you, your deeds.
Let there be no argument between us and you.
God will bring us all together, and with Him is all journeys' end."

[42:15]

135

If God were to bestow abundant sustenance on His servants
they would surely go beyond bounds throughout the earth;
but He sends it down in appropriate measure as He wills:
for of His servants He is Fully-aware, All-seeing.
He is the One Who sends down rain
after they have lost all hope
and unfolds His Grace.
And He is the Protector, the One Worthy of all Praise.

[42:27-28]

Whatever you are given here is for the convenience of this Life:
but that which is with God is better and more enduring—
for those who have faith and put their trust in their Sustainer;
those who avoid the greater crimes and shameful deeds
and when they are angry, even then forgive;
those who pay attention to their Instructor and are constant in prayer;
who conduct their affairs by mutual consultation;
and who give out of the sustenance We bestow on them.

[42:36-38]

And so We have by Our Command sent inspiration to you:
you did not know what revelation was or what faith was;
but We have made the Qurʾān a Light
with which We guide such of Our servants as We will;
and truly you are guiding to the Straight Way,
the Way of God
to Whom belongs whatever is in the heavens and whatever is on earth:
witness how all affairs incline towards God!

[42:52-53]

Gold

ʾAz-Zukhruf

When Jesus came with clear signs he said:
"Now I have come to you with wisdom
and in order to make clear to you
some of that about which you differ.
So remain conscious of God and heed me.
For God, He is my Sustainer and your Sustainer,
so worship Him: this is a Straight Way."

[43:63-64]

Except for the righteous,
friends on that Day will be enemies to one another.
O devoted ones! no fear shall be with you that Day
nor shall you grieve—
those who have had faith in Our signs and have bowed in surrender.
Enter the Garden, you and your spouses, rejoicing.
To them will be passed around dishes and goblets of gold;
there will be there all that their souls could desire,
all that could delight their eyes;
and you shall abide there.
Such will be the Garden of which you are made heirs
for your good deeds.
There you shall have abundant fruit
from which you shall have contentment.

[43:67-73]

Smoke

ʾAd-Dukhān

Ha Mim.[58]
By the Book that makes things clear—
We sent it down during a blessed night:
for We wish to give counsel.
In wisdom, that night the distinction between all things is clarified,
by command from Our Presence.
For We always are sending guidance
as a mercy from your Sustainer:
for He/She alone is All-hearing, All-Seeing;
the Sustainer of the heavens and the earth
and all between them, if only you have inner certainty.
There is no god but He/She: it is He/She Who gives life and gives death,
your Sustainer and the Sustainer of your earliest ancestors.

[44:1-9]

---

[58] See note 40.

The Kneeling

ʾAl-Jāthiyah

It is God Who has made the sea in service to you
that ships may sail through it by His command
that you may seek His abundance and that you may be grateful.
And He has made in service to you as a gift from Him
all that is in the heavens and on earth:
witness, truly, in that are signs for those who reflect.
Tell those who have faith to forgive
those who do not consider the coming of the Days of God:
it is for Him to recompense each People
according to what they have earned.
If anyone does a righteous deed it is to his/her own benefit;
if he/she does harm it works against his/her own soul.
In the end you will all be brought back to your Sustainer.

[45:12-15]

Then We put you on the path of the Way:
so follow that
and do not follow the desires of those who have no knowledge.
They could be of no use to you against God:
those who do wrong have only each other as protectors,
but God is the Protector of the righteous.
These are clear signs to all people
and a guidance and mercy to those endowed with inner certainty.

[45:18-20]

The Sand-Dunes

ʾAl-ʾAḥqāf

Truly those who say, "Our Sustainer is God"
and remain steadfast—
no fear shall they have, neither shall they grieve.
These shall be companions of the Garden, dwelling there
as a completion for their deeds.
We have enjoined on the human being kindness to his parents:
in pain did his mother bear him and in pain did she give him birth.
The carrying of the child to his weaning is thirty months.
At length when he reaches the age of maturity
and attains forty years he prays, "O my Sustainer!
Inspire me to be grateful for Your blessings
which You have bestowed on me and on both my parents
and that I may act rightly in a way which You may approve;
and be gracious to me in my offspring.
Truly, I have turned to you, and truly, I bow in surrender."
Such are they from whom We shall accept the best of their deeds
and disregard their mistakes:
they shall be among the companions of the Garden:
this is a true promise made to them.

[46:13-16]

Muḥammad

O you who have faith!
if you will help God,
He will help you and secure your footing.

[47:7]

To those who receive guidance, He increases their guidance
and causes them to grow in God-consciousness.

[47:17]

The life of this world is just a play and a passing delight,
yet if you have faith and guard against evil
He will grant you your recompense
and will not ask you for all your possessions.
If He were to ask you for all of them and press you,
you would grasp them more tightly,
and He would elicit all your ill-feeling.
Witness that you are those invited to spend freely in the Way of God;
but among you are some who are stingy.
But any who are stingy are so at the expense of their own souls.
But God is free of all wants and it is you who are needy.

[47:36-38]

Victory

ʾAl-Fateḥ

It is He Who sent down tranquillity
into the hearts of the faithful
so that they may add faith to their faith;
for to God belong the forces of the heavens and the earth;
and God is All-Knowing, All-Wise.

[48:4]

For to God belong the forces of the heavens and the earth;
and God is Almighty, All-Wise.
We have truly sent you as a witness, as a bringer of joyful news,
and as a warner:
so that you, O people, may have faith in God and His Messenger,
that you might assist and honor God
and celebrate His praises morning and evening.

Truly those who pledge their loyalty to you
do no less than pledge their loyalty to God.
The Hand of God is over their hands.
Then anyone who violates their oath
does so to the harm of their own soul
and anyone who remains true to what he/she has pledged to God,
God will grant them a supreme recompense.

[48:7-10]

The blind are not to blame,
nor are the lame to blame,
nor is one who is ill;
but the one who pays attention to God and His Messenger,
God will admit him to gardens beneath which rivers flow;
and the one who turns away,
He will chastise with a sorrowful chastisement.

[48:17]

It is He Who has sent His Messenger with guidance
and the Way of Truth,
so that it might prevail over all false ways;
and God is sufficient as witness.
Muhammad is the Messenger of God;
and those who are with him stand firm
when facing those who deny the Truth,
and are compassionate with each other.
You can see them bow and prostrate themselves in prayer,
seeking grace from God and His good pleasure.
On their faces are their marks, traced by prostration.
This is their parable in the Torah,
and their parable in the Gospel:
like a seed which sends forth its shoot, which grows strong,
so that it becomes thick, and then stands firm on its stem,
delighting those who sow with wonder.
And through them the deniers are confounded.
God has promised those among them who have faith
and do righteous deeds forgiveness and a supreme reward.

[48:27-29]

Inner Rooms

ʾAl-Ḥujurāt

Those who lower their voice in the presence of God's Messenger,
their hearts God has tested for consciousness of Himself:
theirs shall be forgiveness and a great reward.
Those who shout out to you from outside the Inner Rooms,
most of them lack understanding.
If only they had patience until you could come out to them
it would be best for them.
Yet God is Often-Forgiving, Most Merciful.

[49:3-5]

And know that among you is God's Messenger:
were he in many matters to follow your inclinations,
you would surely fall into misfortune;
but God has caused faith to be dear to you,
and has made it beautiful within your hearts,
and He has made hateful to you lack of faith, wickedness,
and rebellion against that which is good.
Such indeed are those who walk in righteousness—
through God's grace and favor;
and God is All-Knowing, Truly Wise.

[49:7-8]

145

The faithful are but a single brotherhood.
So make peace between your two contending siblings,
and remain conscious of God
so that you may be graced with God's Mercy.

[49:10]

O you who have faith!
Do not let some men among you laugh at others;
it may be that the others are better than they.
Nor let some women laugh at others;
it may be that the others are better than they.
Nor speak ill nor with sarcasm towards each other,
nor call each other by taunting names:
a name connoting wickedness
is inappropriate after one has come to faith,
and those who do not stop are doing wrong.
O you who have attained to faith!
As much as you can, avoid suspicion,
for suspicion in some cases is a sin;
and do not spy on each other,
nor speak ill of one another behind each other's backs.
Would any of you like to eat the flesh of his dead brother?
No, you would detest it . . . but remain conscious of God:
for truly, God is Ever Turning One Towards Repentance,
Infinitely Merciful.
O humankind! We created you all out of a male and a female,
and made you into nations and tribes
that you might come to know each other.
Truly, the most highly regarded of you in the sight of God
is the one who does the most good.
And God is All-knowing and is Well-aware of all things.

[49:11-13]

Qāf [59]

Don't they look at the sky above them?
How We have made it and adorned it
and how there are no flaws in it?
And the earth—We have spread it wide
and firmly established mountains on it
and caused it to bring forth every kind of beautiful growth,
so offering an insight and a reminder
to every human being who willingly turns to God.
And We send down from the sky rain charged with blessing
and with it cause gardens to grow, and fields of grain,
and tall palm-trees with their thickly-clustered dates,
as sustenance for human beings;
and by all this We bring dead land to life:
even so will be the Resurrection.

[50:6-11]

It was We who created the human being
and We know what his inmost self whispers within him,
for We are nearer to him than his jugular vein.
Whenever the two demands of his nature come face to face,
contending from the right and the left,
not a word does he utter but there is a watcher with him, ever-present.
And the twilight of death will bring truth before his eyes:
"This was that from which you were looking away!"
And the trumpet shall be blown:
that will be the Day of warning fulfilled.
And every soul will come forward;
with each will be his inner motivations and an inner witness.
And it will be said: "Unmindful you have been,
but now We have lifted from you your veil
and sharp is your sight this day!"

[50:16-22]

And paradise will be brought near to the God-conscious,
no longer will it be distant:
"This is what was promised for you—
to everyone who would turn to God
and keep Him/Her always in remembrance—
who stood in awe of the Most Compassionate though unseen
and brought a heart turned in devotion to Him/Her;
Enter here in peace and security; this is the Day of eternal Life!"
There will be for them there all that they may wish
and yet more in Our Presence.

Bear then with patience all that they say
and celebrate the praises of your Sustainer
before the rising of the sun and before its setting
and in the night also celebrate His/Her praises
and at the end of prostration.
And listen for the Day
when the Caller will call out from a place quite near.

Faṣbir ʿalā mā yaqūlūna wa sabbiḥ
biḥamdi rabbika
qabla tulūʿish shamsi wa qablal ghuruub.
Wa minal layli fasabbiḥehu
wa adbāras sujuud.
Wastamiʿ yawma yunādil munādi mim makānin qareeb.

[50:31-35;39-41]

The Dust-Scattering Winds

ʾAzh-zhāriyāt

Consider the winds that scatter the dust far and wide,
   and those that lift and bear away heavy burdens,
   and those that flow with ease and gentleness,
     and those that distribute by command —
    truly, that which you are promised is true;
    and, truly, judgement must come to pass.

[51:1-6]

Witness: the God-conscious will be amid gardens and springs,
   taking joy in that which their Sustainer gives them
   because before then they had lived a good life:
    they would sleep only a little at night
and from the core of their hearts they would pray for forgiveness;
  and of all that they possessed would grant a rightful share
  to the one who asked and the one who was not able.
  On the earth are signs for those with inner certainty,
  just as within your own selves: will you not then see?
     And in heaven is your sustenance
    and all that which you are promised.
Then by the Sustainer of heaven and earth, this is the Truth—
  as true as the fact that you are able to speak.

[51:15-23]

We have built the universe with skill and power;
and truly, it is We Who are steadily expanding it.
And We have spread wide the earth—
how well We have ordered it!
And of everything, We have created opposites
that you might bear in mind that God alone is One.
And so, say, "Hasten to God.
Truly, I am but a warner to you from Him.
And do not attribute partners to God:
I am clearly a warner to you from Him."

[51:47-51]

Yet go on reminding: for reminding benefits the faithful.
And I have created the invisible beings and human beings
only that they may worship Me.
No sustenance do I require of them
nor do I require that they should feed Me.
For God is the Giver of All Sustenance,
the Lord of All Power, the Eternally Steadfast.

[51:55-58]

Mount Sinai

ʾAṭ-Ṭūr

By the Mount,
by revelation inscribed
in unfolding scrolls,
by the long-enduring House,[60]
by the Canopy raised high,
and by the swelling Ocean,
truly, the judgement decreed by your Sustainer
will indeed come to pass.
No one can turn it aside.

[52:1-8]

And those who have faith
and whose families follow them in faith,
We shall unite them with their families;
and We shall not let anything of their work go to waste:
each human being will be held in pledge for his own deeds.

[52:21]

Now await in patience the command of your Sustainer:
for truly you are within Our sight.
And celebrate the praises of your Sustainer
whenever you arise,
and for part of the night also praise Him/Her
and at the retreat of the stars!

[52:48-49]

---

[60]House of worship: a metaphor for the heart of the faithful one, the place where
one is closest to God.

The Star

'An-Najm [61]

Consider this star as it descends from on high.
Your companion is neither astray nor deluded,
nor does he speak by his own desire.
It is no less than inspiration sent down to him:
he was taught by one mighty in power, endowed with wisdom, [62]
who manifested himself in his true nature,
appearing in the highest part of the horizon;
then he approached and came close,
until he was but two bow-lengths apart or nearer.
And so God revealed to His servant
that which He considered right to convey.
In no way did the heart deny that which he saw.
Will you then dispute with him concerning what he saw?
For indeed he saw him a second time
near the Lote-tree beyond which none may pass,
near which is the garden of promise.
Behold, the Lote-tree was veiled in a veil of nameless splendor;
his eye never wavered nor did it stray!
For truly did he see the finest signs of his Sustainer!

[53:1-18]

---

[61] *Najm* is also the word for unfolding; something that appears gradually.
[62] This instructor is understood to be the angel Gabriel, the Angel of Revelation, who appeared to Muhammad.

152

And so turn away from those who turn from Our Message
desiring nothing but the life of this world.
That is as much as they know.
Truly, your Sustainer knows best who strays from His path
and He knows best who follows His guidance.
For to God belongs all that is in the heavens and on earth;
so that He rewards those who do evil according to their deeds,
and He rewards those who do good with what is best.
As for those who avoid the grave sins and shameful deeds,
though occasionally they may stumble—
truly, your Sustainer is vast in forgiveness.
He knows you well when He brings you out of the earth
and when you are hidden in your mother's wombs;
so do not claim purity for yourselves—
He knows best who is conscious of Him.

[53:29-32]

Is he not acquainted with what is in the books of Moses
and of Abraham who was true to his trust?
Namely that no bearer of burdens can bear the burden of another;
that the human being can have nothing but that for which he strives;
that in time his striving will become apparent;
and then he will be recompensed
with the most complete recompense;
that to your Sustainer is the final Goal;
that it is He alone who causes your laughter and your tears;
that it is He Who grants death and life;
that He created in pairs, male and female,
from a drop of sperm as it is poured forth;
and that with Him rests another coming to life;
that it is He Who gives wealth and contentment;
and that it is He alone Who sustains the brightest star.[63]

[53:36-49]

---

[63]Sirius, of the constellation Canis Major, the brightest star in the heavens. This
phrase might also be understood as, "it is God alone who sustains the brightest of
the saints, those who shine with His Light."

The Moon

ʾAl-Qamar

Long before, the people of Noah called it a lie:
they denied Our servant and said, "He is mad!"
and he was driven out.
Then he called upon his Sustainer:
"I am overcome, O come then to my aid!"
So We opened the gates of heaven with water pouring forth.
And We caused the earth to gush with springs,
so that the waters met for the determined purpose.
But We carried him
on that vessel made of planks, caulked with palm-fiber.
Under Our eyes it floated:
a recompense for one who had been rejected ungratefully!
And forever We have left this as a sign:
who then will take it to heart?

[54:9-15]

And We have indeed made the Qurʾān easy
to understand and remember:
who then is willing to take it to heart?

[54:17]

The Infinitely Compassionate

ʾAr-Raḥmān

The Most Gracious!
It is He Who has taught the Qurʾān.
He has created the human being.
He has taught them clear thought and speech.
The sun and the moon follow their designated paths;
and the herbs and the trees—both bow in adoration.
And He has raised high the heavens,
and He has devised a balance
so that you might not measure wrongly.
So weigh justly and don't measure lightly.
And the earth He has outspread for all creatures
with fruit on it and date-palms bearing enclosed clusters
and grain on tall stalks and sweetly fragrant plants;
which then of your Sustainer's blessings will you deny?

[55:1-13]

He is the Instructor of the two places of sunrise,
and the Instructor of the two places of sunset.
Then which of your Sustainer's blessings will you deny?
He has given freedom to the two great bodies of water
so that they might meet:
yet between them is a threshold which they cannot cross.
Then which of your Sustainer's blessings will you deny?
Out of these come pearls and coral.
Then which of your Sustainer's blessings will you deny?
And His are the ships sailing smoothly, lofty as mountains,
through the seas.
Then which of your Sustainer's blessings will you deny?
All that is on earth will perish;
but forever will abide the Face of your Sustainer,
Full of Majesty and Abundant Honor.
Then which of your Sustainer's blessings will you deny?
Every creature in the heavens and on earth depends on Him:
every day He manifests in wondrous new ways!
Then which of your Sustainer's blessings will you deny?

[55:17-30]

Is there any reward for good other than good?
Then which of your Sustainer's blessings will you deny?

[55:60-61]

156

That Which Must Come to Pass

ʾAl-Wāqiʿah

Do you see the seed that you sow in the ground?
Is it you that causes it to grow or are We the cause?
Were it Our Will we could crumble it to dry powder
and you would be left in awe,
lamenting: "We are ruined; we've been deprived."
Have you ever considered the water which you drink?
Do you bring it down from the clouds or do We?
Were it Our will We could make it salty and bitter:
why, then, aren't you grateful?
Have you ever considered the fire which you kindle?
Is it you who have brought into being the tree
which feeds the fire, or is it We Who cause it to grow?
It is We Who have made it a reminder
and a comfort for those who wander in the wilderness.
Then celebrate the limitless glory
of the Name of your Sustainer, the Most High.

[56:63–74]

Iron

ʾAl-Ḥadīd

Whatever is in the heavens and on earth
let it declare the praises and glory of God:
for God alone is almighty, truly wise.
To God belongs the dominion of the heavens and the earth;
it is God Who gives life and bestows death;
and God has power over all things.
God is the First and the Last, the Manifest and the Hidden,
and knows completely all things.
It is God Who created the heavens and the earth in six aeons
and is firmly settled on the throne of power.

God knows all that enters within the earth
and all that comes forth out of it,
as well as all that descends from heaven
and all that ascends to it.
And God is with you wherever you may be
and sees well all that you do.
To God belongs the dominion of the heavens and the earth.
And all things return to God
Who merges night into day and merges day into night
and knows completely the secrets of hearts.

[57:1-6]

It is God Who sends to His servants clear signs
that He may lead you out of the depths of darkness
into the Light.
And truly, God is to you Most Kind and Merciful.

[57:9]

Who will loan to God a beautiful loan?
For God will increase it many times to his/her credit
and he/she will have a generous recompense.
One Day you will see the faithful men and the faithful women,
how their Light runs forward before them and to their right:
"Good news for you today: gardens beneath which running waters flow,
where you may live—this, this is the highest achievement!"

[57:11-12]

Hasn't the time come for the faithful
that their hearts in all humility
should engage in the remembrance of God
and of the truth which has been revealed,
and that they should not become like those
to whom revelation was given but whose hearts have hardened
with the passing of time
so that many among them now rebel
against that which is right?
Know that God gives life to the earth after it has been lifeless!
We have indeed made Our signs clear to you
that you might learn wisdom.

[57:16-17]

Don't despair over things that pass you by
nor exult over blessings that come to you.
For God does not love those who are conceited and boastful,
those who are grasping and encourage others to be greedy.
And as for the one who turns his back—
truly, God alone is Self-Sufficient,
the One to Whom All Praise Is Due.
We have sent our messengers with clear signs,
and through them We bestowed revelation and a balance
so that people might behave with justice;
and We sent down iron in which is awesome power
as well as many benefits for humankind,
that God might test who it is that will help unseen
Him and His messengers;
for truly, God is the Lord of All Power, Almighty.

[57:23-25]

O you who have attained to faith!
Remain conscious of God and have faith in His messenger,
and He will grant you a double portion of His Mercy:
He will provide for you a light by which you shall walk,
and He will forgive you:
For God is Ever Ready to Forgive and is the Most Merciful.

[57:28]

The Pleading

ʾAl-Mujādilah

Don't you see that God knows all
that is in the heavens and on earth?
There is not a secret consultation between three
but He/She makes the fourth among them,
nor between five but He/She makes the sixth,
nor between fewer nor more but He/She is in their midst
wherever they may be:
in the end He/She will show them the truth of their actions,
on the Day of Reckoning,
for God has full knowledge of all things.

[58:7]

The Gathering

ʾAl-Ḥashr

Those saved from the covetousness of their own souls,
they are the ones who achieve prosperity.

[59:9]

O you who have attained to faith!
Remain conscious of God,
and let every soul look to what he/she has prepared for the day to come.
And remain conscious of God:
for God is well-aware of all that you do.
And do not be like those who forget God,
whom He then causes to forget their own souls!

[59:18-19]

Had We sent down this Qurʾān on a mountain,
truly, you would have seen it humble itself and break apart
out of awe of God—
such are the parables which We offer to human beings
that they might reflect.

[59:21]

God is He other than Whom there is no god,
Who knows what is hidden and what is manifest;
Hu,[64] the Infinitely Compassionate, the Infinitely Merciful.
God is He other than Whom there is no god,
the Sovereign, the Holy One, the Source of Peace,
the Inspirer of Faith, the Preserver of Security,
the Exalted in Might, the Compelling, the Supreme:
Glory to God!
Who is above the partners they attribute to Him
He is God, the Creator, the Evolver, the Bestower of Forms.
To Hu belong the Most Beautiful Names:
whatever is in the heavens and on earth
declares His Praises and Glory,
and He is the exalted in Might, the All-Wise.

Huwallāhullazhī laa 'ilāha 'illā Huu;
'Ālimul ghaybi wash-shahādati
Huwar Raḥmānur Raḥeem.
Huwallāhullazhī laa 'ilāha 'illā Huu;
'Al Malikul Quddūsus Salāmul
Mu'minul Muhayminul
'Azīzul Jabbārul Mutakabbir.
Subḥānallāhi 'ammā yushrikuun.
Huwallāhul Khāliqul Bāri'ul Muṣawwiru
lahul 'asmaa'ul ḥusnaa.
Yusabbiḥu lahu mā fissamāwāti wal 'arḍi
wa Huwal 'Azīzul Ḥakeem.

[59:22-24]

The One Who Is Tested

ʾAl-Mumtaḥanah

"O our Sustainer, in You we have placed our trust
and to You we turn in repentance:
for with You is all journeys' end.
O our Sustainer! Do not make us a ploy
for those who deny the Truth,
but forgive us, O our Sustainer!
For You are the Almighty, the Truly-Wise."

(prayer of Abraham and his followers)

Rabbanā ʿalayka tawakkalnā
wa ʾilayka ʾanabnā
wa ʾilaykal maṣeer.
Rabbanā lā tafʿalnā fitnatal-
lillazhīna kafaru
waghfir lanā Rabbanaa
ʾInnaka ʾAntal ʿAzīzul Ḥakeem

[60:4–5]

The Ranks

ʾAṣ-Ṣaff

Whatever is in the heavens and on earth,
let it declare the praises and glory of God:
for He is the Exalted in Might, the All-Wise.
O you who have faith! Why do you say that which you do not do?
It is most displeasing in God's sight
that you say that which you do not do.

[61:1–3]

That you have faith in God and His messenger,
and that you strive in God's cause
with your possessions and your lives:
that is best for you, if only you knew!

[61:11]

165

The Assembly[65]

ʾAl-Jumuʿah

O faithful ones!
When the call to prayer is proclaimed on the day of assembly
hasten earnestly to the remembrance of God
and leave aside your business and trade:
that is best for you if only you knew!
And when the prayer is completed,
then you may move about through the land
and seek out God's abundance:
and remember God often
that you may attain felicity.
But when they catch sight of some bargain or diversion,
they head off towards that and leave you standing.
Say: "That which is from the Presence of God is better
than any bargain or passing delight!
For God is the best of providers."

[62:9-11]

---

[65] The gathering for prayer.

The Hypocrites

ʾAl-Munāfiqūn

O faithful ones!
Do not let your possessions or your children
distract you from the remembrance of God.
If anyone acts like that the loss is their own.
And give something
out of the sustenance which We have bestowed on you
before death approaches one among you and he/she should say:
"O my Lord! Why don't you give me a little while longer,
that I might then be generous and charitable
and be among those who do good?"
But to no soul will God grant a further time
when the appointed time has come:
and God is fully aware of all that you do.

[63:9-11]

Loss and Gain

ʾAt-Taghābun

Whatever is in the heavens and on earth
declares the praises and glory of God:
to Hu[66] belongs all sovereignty and to Hu belongs all praise,
and Hu has power over all things.
It is He Who has created you;
and among you there are some who deny the Truth
and some who are faithful;
and God sees well all that you do.
He has created the heavens and the earth in accordance with Truth
and has shaped you and made your shapes beautiful;
and with Him is your journey's end.
He knows what is in the heavens and on earth;
He knows what you conceal and what you reveal:
yes, God knows well the secrets of hearts.

[64:1-4]

---

[66] See note 30.

Divorce

ʾAṭ-Ṭalāq

For the one who remains conscious of God;
He always prepares a way of emergence
and He provides for him/her in ways he/she could never imagine.
And if anyone puts his/her trust in God, sufficient is God for him/her.
For God will surely accomplish His purpose:
truly, for all things has God appointed an appropriate measure.

[65:2-3]

Let the person of means spend according to his/her means:
and the one whose resources are restricted,
let him/her spend according to that which God has given.
God puts no burden on any soul beyond what He/She bestows.
Surely, after hardship God will bring ease.

[65:7]

Prohibition

ʾAt-Taḥrīm

And God sets forth as an example to those who have faith
the wife of Pharaoh:
witness, she said: "O my Sustainer!
Build for me in nearness to You a mansion in the Garden
and save me from Pharaoh and his actions
and save me from those who do wrong";
also Mary, the daughter of 'Imran, who guarded her chastity,
and We breathed into her of Our spirit,
and she witnessed to the truth of the words of her Sustainer
and of His revelations and was one of those devoted.

[66:11-12]

Sovereignty

ʾAl-Mulk

Blessed be the One in Whose hands is sovereignty:
and He/She has power over all things—
He/She Who created death and life
that He/She may test which of you is best in deeds.
And He/She is the Almighty, the One Who is Ever Ready to Forgive,
He/She Who created the seven heavens in harmony;
no lack of proportion will you see
in that which the Most Compassionate has created—
just look again: can you see any flaw?

[67:1-4]

And whether you hide your word or declare it
He/She certainly knows the secrets of hearts.
Should He/She not know, He/She Who created?
And He/She is the Most Subtle,
and the One Who is Aware of Everything.

[67:13-14]

Don't they observe the birds above them
spreading their wings and folding them in?
None can uphold them except the Most Gracious:
truly, it is He/She Who watches over all things.
No; who is there who can stand with you like an army
except the Most Merciful?
Those who deny the Truth are only deluding themselves.
Or who is there who can provide you with sustenance
if He/She were to withhold His/Her provision?

[67:19-21]

The Pen

ʾAl-Qalam

In the Name of God,
the Infinitely Compassionate and Most Merciful.
Nun.[67] By the Pen and by that which they write,
by the grace of your Sustainer, you are not crazy.
And truly, yours is an unceasing recompense:
for surely, yours is a sublime way of life.
Soon you will see and they will see
which of you it is who is without reason.
Truly, your Sustainer knows best
which of you has strayed from His Path,
and He knows best who receives true guidance.
So do not listen to those who deny the Truth.
They want you to compromise,
so that they might also compromise.

[68:1-9]

---

[67] See note 40.

The Laying Bare of the Truth

ʾAl-Ḥāqqah

The certain Truth!
What is the certain Truth?
And what will make you realize what the certain Truth is?

[69:1–3]

And so I call to witness what you see
And what you do not see
that this is truly the word of an honored messenger.
It is not the word of a poet; how little faith you have!
Nor is it the word of a soothsayer;
what little counsel you take to heart.
It is a revelation from the Sustainer of all the Worlds.
And if the messenger were to invent any sayings in Our name
We should certainly seize him by his right hand
and We should certainly then cut off the life-blood of his heart,
nor could any of you save him.
But truly, this is a message for those who stand in awe of God.
And We certainly know that there are among you
those who deny Our signs;
but truly revelation is a source of remorse for the deniers.
And surely it is the certain truth.
So glorify the name of your Sustainer, the Most High.

[69:38–52]

The Ways of Ascent

ʾAl-Maʿārij

Truly the human being was born restless—
filled with self-pity when difficulty touches him
and selfish when good fortune comes to him—
but not those who consciously turn towards God in prayer—
those who continually persist in their prayer,
and in whose wealth is a recognized right
for those who ask and for the one who cannot ask,
and who grasp the truth of the Day of Reckoning.

[70:19-26]

Noah

Nūḥ

We sent Noah to his people, saying:
"Warn your people before grievous suffering comes to them."
He said: "O my People! I am but a plain warner sent to you:
that you should worship God, and stand in awe of Him;
take to heart what I say
so that He may forgive you your mistakes
and grant you ease for a while;
for when the interval given by God is finished
it cannot be extended: if only you knew."

[71:1-4]

"So I've called to them openly,
and I've spoken to them publicly and also in private,
saying: 'Seek the forgiveness of your Sustainer,
for He is the One Who Loves to Forgive;
He will shower you with abundant blessings,
and will strengthen you with wealth and children,
and give you gardens and rivers of flowing water.
What's wrong with you that you don't place your hope
in God's Beneficence,
seeing that it is He Who has created you in successive stages?
Don't you see how God has created the seven heavens in harmony
and made the moon a light in their midst
and made the sun a glorious lamp?
And how God has caused you to grow gradually from the earth,
and in the end He will return you to it
and then raise you forth anew?
And God has unfolded wide the earth for you that you might move about
there on spacious paths.' "

[71:8-20]

The Unseen Beings

ʾAl-Jinn

Say: "It has been revealed to me
that a company of unseen beings listened.
And they said, 'We have truly heard a wondrous recitation![68]
It guides towards consciousness of what is right,
and so we have come to have faith in it.
We shall never attribute divinity
to anyone along with our Sustainer.' "

[72:1-2]

"He is the Knower of the Unseen,
nor does He acquaint anyone with His mysteries
except a messenger whom He has chosen.
And then He sends forth guardians
to precede him and to follow him,
that He may know
that he has delivered the messages of his Sustainer:
for He encompasses all that is with him
and takes account, one by one, of everything."

[72:26-28]

---

[68]Discourse: recitation, Qurʾān

The Covered One

ʾAl-Muzzammil

O you who are covered!
Stand in prayer by night but not all the night—
half of it or a little less,
or a little more; and recite the Qurʾān, slowly and distinctly.
We shall soon send down to you a weighty word.
Truly, the rising by night
is the strongest means of governing the soul
and the most appropriate for Words of prayer.
Truly, by day there is a long chain of duties for you;
but keep in remembrance the name of your Sustainer
and devote yourself to Him wholeheartedly.
Sustainer of the East and the West, there is no god but Hu:[69]
take Hu therefore as the guardian of your affairs.

[73:1-9]

---

[69] See note 30.

Truly, this is a guidance:
so, whoever will, let him set out on a path to his Sustainer!
Your Sustainer knows that you stand forth in prayer
nearly two-thirds of the night
or half the night or a third of the night
and so do some of those with you.
But God Who proportions night and day
knows that you cannot keep count of it,
so He has turned to you in mercy.
Recite, then as much of the Qurʾān as may be easy for you.
He knows that there may be among you some who are not well,
others traveling through the land seeking of God's bounty,
and yet others struggling in God's cause.
So recite then as much of the Qurʾān as may be easy;
and be constant in prayer and spend in charity;
and loan to God a beautiful loan.
And whatever good you send forth for your souls,
you shall find it in God's Presence richer and better in reward.
And always seek God's grace:
for God is Ever Ready to Forgive, Most Merciful.

[73:19-20]

The Enfolded One

ʾAl-Muddath-thir

O you who are enfolded!
Arise and give guidance!
And glorify the greatness of your Sustainer!
And purify your inmost heart!
And turn away from all that is unclean!
And do not expect in giving any increase for yourself!
But for your Sustainer's sake be patient and steadfast!

[74:1-7]

Resurrection

ʾAl-Qiyāmah

I call to witness the Resurrection Day;
and I call to witness the self-reproaching soul!
Do human beings think that We cannot assemble their bones?
Yes, We are able to put together in perfect order
the very tips of their fingers.
But they long for that which is harmful even in the time left to them.
They ask: "When is the Day of Resurrection?"
At length when the eye is dazed and the moon is buried in darkness
and the sun and moon are joined together,
that Day the human being will cry out, "Where is the refuge?"
No, there is no refuge!
With your Sustainer alone will be the place of rest that Day.

[75:1-12]

181

The Human Being

ʾAl-Insān

Has there not been over the human being a long span of time
when he was nothing—not even mentioned?
Truly, We created the human being
from a drop of mingled sperm in order to test him.
So We gave him hearing and sight, We showed him the Way:
it is up to him whether he is grateful or ungrateful.

[76:1-3]

Surely, It is We Who have sent down the Qurʾān to you step by step.
So be constant in patience with the command of your Sustainer
and do not yield to the one who is in error or is ungrateful.
And mention your Sustainer's Name morning and evening,
and during the night prostrate yourself before Him/Her
and praise Him/Her throughout the long night.

[76:23-26]

Truly, this is a reminder
so that whoever wishes may take a path to his/her Teacher.
And you exercise your will because God has willed it.
Truly God is All-Knowing, the Most-Wise.

[76:30-31]

Those Sent Forth

ʾAl-Mursalāt

In the Name of God,
the Infinitely Compassionate and Most Merciful
Consider those sent forth, one following another,
which then blow violently in stormy gales
and scatter far and wide,
separating with discernment,
spreading a reminder,
of freedom from reproof or of caution!
Surely, that which you are promised must come to pass.

[77:1-7]

The Tiding

'An-Naba'

What are they arguing about?
About the Great News,
about which they cannot agree.
Truly they shall soon know!
Truly, they shall soon come to know!
Have We not made the earth as a wide expanse
and the mountains as pegs;
and created you in pairs,
and made your sleep for rest,
and made the night as a covering,
and made the day as means of subsistence?
And have We not built over you the seven heavens
and placed within them a wondrous Light?
And do We not send down from the clouds abundant water
that by it We may produce grain and herbs and lush gardens?
Truly the Day of Sorting Out is something already determined.

[78:1-18]

Those that Rise

ʾAn-Nāziʿāt

Has the story of Moses reached you?
Witness, your Sustainer called to him in the sacred valley of Tuwa:
"Go to Pharaoh
for he has indeed gone beyond all bounds of what is right.
And say to him: 'Would you wish to attain purity?
Then I might guide you to your Sustainer
so that you might stand in awe of Him.' "
He then showed him the Great Sign.
But Pharaoh denied it and rebelled against God;
hastily, he turned his back.
Then he gathered his men and proclaimed,
"I am your Lord Most High."
But God chastised him and made an example of him
in the Hereafter as in this life.
Truly, in this is a teaching, a warning
for whoever remains conscious of God.

[79:15-26]

He Frowned

'Abasa

He[70] frowned and turned away
because the blind man came to him.
But how were you to know whether he might grow in purity,
or whether he might have received counsel
and been helped by this reminder?
And the one who regards himself as self-sufficient,
to him you pay attention;
though if he does not grow in purity you are not to blame.
But as for the one who came eagerly to you
and with an inner awe,
him you disregarded.
By no means should it be so!
For this is indeed a reminder
for anyone who will remember.

[80:1–12]

---

[70]The Prophet Muhammad was involved in conversation with some of the influential people of pagan Mecca, attempting to convey to them the truth of his message when a blind man approached and asked a question of him regarding the Qur'an. Muhammad frowned and turned away from him, annoyed by the interruption. Immediately, Muhammad was reproved by God with these first verses of this *surah* which then took on the title "He frowned."

The Enshrouding

ʾAt-Takwīr

When the sun is enshrouded,
when the stars fall losing their brilliance,
when the mountains vanish,
when pregnant camels are forgotten
and the wild beasts are herded together,
when the oceans surge beyond their bounds,
when every soul joins with its own kind,
when the infant girl who was buried alive is questioned
for what crime she was killed,
when the scrolls are unfolded,
when the heavens are unveiled,
when the blazing fire is kindled bright,
and when the Garden is brought near,
then shall each soul know what it has prepared.

[81:1-14]

So, truly, I call to witness the planets that recede,
go straight, or hide;
and the night as it vanishes,
and the dawn as it breathes the darkness away:
truly, this is the word of a most honorable Messenger.

[81:15-19]

The Rending

ʾAl-ʾInfiṭār

When the sky is rent apart,
when the stars are scattered,
when the oceans burst forth,
and when the graves are turned upside down,
then shall each soul know what it has sent ahead
and what it has kept back.
O human being! What has seduced you
away from your Most Generous Instructor?
The One Who created you,
fashioned you in appropriate proportion,
and gave you a proper inclination:
that One puts you together in whatever form He/She wills.

[82:1-8]

Those Who Give Short Measure

ʾAl-Muṭaffifīn

Woe to those who commerce in fraud,
those who when they are to receive from other people
exact full measure,
but when they must measure out give less than is due.
Do they think they won't be called to account—
on an awesome day,
a day when all humankind will stand
before the Sustainer of all Worlds?

[83:1-6]

The Splitting Asunder

ʾAl-ʾInshiqāqq

When the sky is split apart
in obedience to its Sustainer—and it must—
and when the earth is leveled,
and casts forth what is within it, and becomes utterly empty,
in obedience to its Sustainer—and it must—
O human being! Truly, you are laboring towards your Sustainer,
painfully struggling, but then you shall meet Him/Her.

[84:1-6]

So I call to witness the rosy glow of sunset,
the night and its progression,
and the moon as it grows in fullness;
surely, you shall travel from stage to stage.
What then is the matter with them
that they do not have faith in the unfolding?

[84:16-20]

190

The Great Constellation

ʾAl-Burūj

Truly, your Sustainer's grasp is strong.
It is He Who creates from the very beginning
and it is He Who can restore.
And He is Ever Ready to Forgive, the Loving One,
Lord of the Throne of Glory,
the Unceasing Doer of all that He intends.

[85:12-16]

That Which Comes in the Night

ʾAṭ-Ṭāriq

In the Name of God, the Infinitely Compassionate and Most Merciful
Consider the sky and the night-visitor.
And what will explain to you what the night-visitor is?
It is the star of piercing brightness.
There is no soul that does not have a protector over it.

Bismillāhir Raḥmānir Raḥeem
Was samaaʾi waṭ-ṭāriqq
Wa maa ʾadrāka maṭ-ṭāriqq
ʾAnnajmu-thāqibb
ʾIn kullu nafsil lammā ʿalayhā ḥāfizh.

[86:1-4]

The All-Highest

'Al-'A'lā

Glorify the name of your Sustainer Most High
Who has created and further given order and proportion;
Who has determined the order, and gives guidance;
and Who brings forth the fertile pasture
and then reduces it to darkened stubble.
We shall teach you to remember
so that you shall not forget, except as God wills:
for truly, He knows what is manifest and all that is hidden.
And We will make easy for you the path towards true ease.
So remind in case the reminder may benefit the hearer.
It will be kept in mind by those who stand in awe of God.

[87:2-11]

Those will prosper who purify themselves
and remember the Name of their Sustainer and pray.

Qad 'aflaḥa man tazakkaa.
Wa zhakarasma Rabbihī fa ṣallaa.

[87:14-15]

The Overshadowing Event

ʾAl-Ghāsiyah

Don't they look at the clouds heavy with rain
and how they are created?
And at the sky, how it is raised high?
And at the mountains, how they are firmly settled?
And at the earth how it is outspread?
So give counsel, for you are one to counsel;
you are not meant to compel them.

[88:17-22]

The Break of Day

ʾAl-Fajr

By the break of day,[71]
by the ten nights;
by the pairs and the One;
and by the night when it passes away,
is there not in these counsel for those who understand?

[89:1–5]

---

[71] This breaking of day indicates the breaking open of the Light of spiritual awakening and the passing of the dark night of doubt and confusion in recognition of the One and creation. It is during the last ten nights of the month of Ramadan that the Night of Power when the Qurʾān began to be received by Muhammad is commemorated. Also, another of the major processes of the Islamic Tradition, the Hajj, takes place during the first ten days and nights of the month of Dhul-Hijja.

194

Now as for man, when his Sustainer tests him,
honoring him with gifts, he boasts: "My Lord has honored me,"
but when He tests him with scarcity,
then he moans, "My Sustainer has disgraced me!"
But no! You don't honor the orphans!
Nor do you encourage one another to feed the poor!
And you greedily devour inheritance.
And you love wealth with undue love!
No! When the earth is crushed to dust,
and your Sustainer comes and His angels rank upon rank,
and the Fire that Day is brought face to face,
on that Day the human being will remember,
but what use will it be then?
He will say: "Oh! How I wish that I had prepared better for this Life."

[89:15-24]

But to the righteous soul will be said:
"O soul in complete rest and satisfaction!
Return to your Sustainer well-pleased and well-pleasing!
Enter then among my devoted ones!
Yes, enter my Garden!"

Yaa 'ayyatuhan nafsul muṭema 'innatu
'irji'ee 'ilā Rabbiki rāḍiyatam marḍiyyah.
Fadekhulī fī 'ibādee.
Wadekhulī jannatee.

[89:27-30]

The Land

ʾAl-Balad

I call to witness this land
in which you are free to dwell,
and the bond between parent and child:
truly, We have created the human being to labor and struggle.
Does he think that no one has power over him?
He may boast: "I have spent abundant wealth!"
Does he think that no one sees him?
Haven't We made a pair of eyes for him?
And a tongue and a pair of lips?
And shown him the two ways?
But he has not quickened along the path that is steep.
And what will explain to you what the steep path is?—
the freeing of one who is enslaved,
or the giving of food in time of need
to the orphan with claims of relationship,
or to the helpless, lowly one in the dust,
and being of those who have faith and encourage patience,
and who encourage deeds of kindness and compassion.
These are the companions of the right hand.

[90:2-18]

The Sun

ʾAsh-Shams

Consider the sun and its splendor,
and the moon as she follows.
Consider the day as it reveals this world,
and the night as it conceals it.
Consider the scope of the heavens
and its wondrous structure;
consider the earth and its broad expanse.
Consider the soul and the order and proportion given to it,
and its enlightenment as to that which is wrong and right:
truly, the one who purifies it shall reach a happy state
and the one who corrupts it shall truly be lost!

Wash shamsi wa ḍuḥāhaa.
Wal qamari izhā talāhaa.
Wan nahāri izhā jal lāhaa.
Wal layli izhā yagh-shāhaa.
Was samaaʾi wa mā banāhaa.
Wal arḍi wa mā ṭaḥāhaa.
Wa nafsin wa mā saw-wāhaa.
Fa ʾalhamahā fujūrahā wa taqwāhaa.
Qad ʾaflaḥa man zakāhaa.
Wa qad khāba man dasāhaa.

[91:1–10]

The Night

ʾAl-Layl

In the Name of God,
the Infinitely Compassionate and Most Merciful
Consider the night as it conceals
and the brilliance of the day;
consider the creation of male and female;
truly, your aims are diverse.
So the one who gives and stands in awe of God
and sincerely affirms that which is best,
We will indeed ease for him/her the path to bliss.
But the one who greedily withholds what is given,
considering himself/herself self-sufficient,
and betrays the good,
We will indeed ease for him/her the path to misfortune;
nor will his/her wealth be of use to him/her when he/she falls.
In truth, it is up to Us to guide,
and truly, to Us belong the End and the Beginning.

[92:1-13]

The Glorious Morning Light

ʾAḍ-Ḍuḥā

In the Name of God,
the Infinitely Compassionate and Most Merciful
By the glorious morning light
and by the night when it is still
Your Sustainer has not forgotten you, nor is He displeased.
And, truly, that which comes after will be better for you than the present.
And soon your Sustainer will give
that with which you will be content.
Didn't He find you an orphan and shelter you?
Didn't He find you wandering and guide you?
Didn't He find you in need and satisfy your need?
So do not be harsh with orphans,
nor turn away one who asks something of you,
but continually declare the blessings of your Sustainer!

Bismillāhir Raḥmānir Raḥeem
Waḍ-ḍuḥaa. Wal layli ʾizhā sajaa.
Mā wad daʿaka rabbuka wa mā qalaa.
Wa lal ʾākhiratu khayrul laka minal ʾūlaa.
Wa lasawfa yuʿṭīka rabbuka fatarḍaa.
ʾAlam yajideka yatīman fa ʾāwaa.
Wa wajadaka ḍaal-lan fahadaa.
Wa wajadaka ʿaaʾilan fa ʾaghnaa.
Fa ʾammal yatīma falā taqhar.
Wa ʾammas saaʾila falā tanhar.
Wa ʾammā bi niʿmati rabbika faḥadith.

[93:1-11]

The Expansion

ʾAl-Inshirāḥ

Have We not expanded your chest,[72]
and removed from you the burden
which weighed down your back,
and increased your remembrance?
So, truly, with every difficulty comes ease;
truly, with every difficulty comes ease.
So when you are free from your task continue to strive,
and to your Sustainer turn with loving attention.

ʾAlam nashraḥ laka ṣadrak.
Wa waḍaʿnā ʿanka wizrak.
ʾAllazhee ʾanqaḍa zhahrak.
Wa rafaʿnā laka zhikrak.
Faʾinna maʿal ʿusri yusraa.
ʾInna maʿal ʿusri yusraa.
Faʾizhā faraghta fanṣabb.
Wa ʾilā rabbika farghabb.

[94:1–8]

---

[72] And so allowing space for the opening of the heart. It is reported that the angel Gabriel appeared to the Prophet Muhammad, opened his chest, and removed the impurities remaining in his heart.

The Fig

'At-Tīn

By the fig and the olive,
and Mount Sinai,
and this city of security,[73]
truly, We have created human beings in the best proportion.
Then We reduce them to the lowest of the low
except those who have faith and act rightly:
for they shall have an unceasing reward.
Then what after this can turn you away from this Way?
Is God not the wisest of judges?

Wattīni waz zaytuun.
Wa ṭūri sīneen.
Wa hāzhal baladil 'ameen.
Laqad khalaqnal 'innsāna fee 'ahsani taqweem.
Thumma radadnāhu 'asfala sāfileen.
'Illālazhīna 'āmanu wa 'amilussālihāti
falahum 'ajrun ghayru mamnuun.
Famā yukazhibuka ba'du biddeen.
'Alaysallāhu bi 'ahkamil hākimeen.

[95:1–8]

---

[73]The fig, and the olive, Mount Sinai and the City of Security (Mecca) are representative of the major prophets of the Abrahamic tradition and also the aspects of the human being that have the capacity to receive revelation.

The Connecting Cell

'Al-'Alaq

In the Name of God, the Infinitely Compassionate and Most Merciful
Recite! In the name of your Sustainer Who created,
created the human being out of a connecting cell:
Recite! And your Sustainer is the Most Generous,
the One Who taught by the pen,
taught humankind what it did not know.
No, but humankind goes beyond all bounds
when it considers itself self-sufficient.
In truth, to their Sustainer all will return.

Bismillāhir Raḥmānir Raḥeem
'Iqra' bismi rabbikal lazhī khalaq.
Khalaqal 'innsāna min 'alaq.
'Iqra' wa rabbukal 'akram.
'Allazhī 'allama bil qalam.
'Allamal 'innsāna mā lam y'alam.
Kallaa 'innal 'innsāna layaṭghaa.
'Ar ra'āhus staghnaa.
'Inna 'ilā rabbikar ruj'aa.

[96:1–8]

Bow down in adoration and draw near!
Wasjud waq-taribb

[96:19]

The Night of Power[74]

ʾAl-Qadr

In the Name of God,
the Infinitely Compassionate and Most Merciful
We have indeed revealed this during the Night of Power.
And what will explain to you what the Night of Power is?
The Night of Power is better than a thousand months.
Within it the angels descend bearing divine inspiration
by God's permission upon every mission:
Peace! . . . This until the rise of dawn!

Bismillāhir Raḥmānir Raḥeem
ʾInnaa ʾanzalnāhu fī laylatil qadr.
Wa maa ʾadrāka mā laylatul qadr.
Laylatul qadri khayrum min ʾalfi shahr.
Tanaz zalul malaa ʾikatu war rūḥu
fīhā bi ʾizhni rabbihim min kulli ʾamr.
Salāmun hiya ḥattā maṭlaʿil fajr.

[97:1-5]

---

[74] The night during which the Prophet Muhammad received the first revelation. Tradition reports that historically it was one of the last ten nights of the month of Ramadan, probably the 27th. The Night of Power is a night when inspiration arrives and closeness with one's Sustainer. One must be watchful for its coming.

Clear Evidence

ʾAl-Bayyinah

In the Name of God, the Infinitely Compassionate and Most Merciful
Those who deny Truth—from among the People of the Book[75]
and among those who attribute divinity to anything beside God—
would never be left to themselves
until after there should come to them clear evidence—
a messenger from God conveying revelations blessed with purity,
within which are true and straight laws.
Nor did the People of the Book break up their unity
until after there came to them clear evidence.
And yet they have been commanded no more than this:
to worship God, sincere in their devoted faith in Him alone;
to remain constant in prayer; and to practice regular charity;
and that is the True and Straight Way.
Those who deny Truth among the People of the Book
and among those who attribute divinity to anything beside God
will find themselves in the fire, dwelling there.
They are the worst of creatures.
Those who have faith and do righteous deeds—
it is they who are the best of creatures.
Their recompense is with God:
gardens of perpetual felicity beneath which rivers flow—
they will dwell there forever;
God well-pleased with them and they with Him:
all this for those who stand in awe of their Sustainer.

[98:1-8]

---

[75] Those who have followed revelation received by the prophets.

The Earthquake

'Az-Zalzalah

In the Name of God
the Infinitely Compassionate and Most Merciful
When the earth shakes with her final convulsion,
and the earth yields up her burdens,
and the human being cries out: "What is the matter with her?"
On that Day she will declare her tidings:
your Sustainer will have inspired her.
On that Day all human beings will come forward separately
to be shown their deeds.
Then shall anyone who has done an atom's weight of good see it!
And anyone who has done an atom's weight of harm shall see that.

Bismillāhir Raḥmānir Raheem
'Izhā zulzilatil 'arḍu zilzālahaa.
Wa 'akhrajatil 'arḍu 'athqālahaa.
Wa qālal 'innsānu mā lahaa.
Yawma 'izhin tuḥaddithu 'akhbārahaa.
Bi 'anna rabbaka 'awḥā lahaa.
Yawma 'izhin yaṣdurun nāsu 'ashtātal liyuraw 'a'mālahum.
Faman ya'mal mithqāl zharratin khayran yarah.
Wa man ya'mal mithqāl zharratin sharan yarah.

[99:1–8]

Those that Run

ʾAl-ʿĀdiyāt

In the Name of God,
the Infinitely Compassionate and Most Merciful
By those that run, panting and sparking fire,
charging at daybreak,
and raising clouds of dust,
and penetrating deep into the enemy,
truly, human beings are ungrateful to their Sustainer;
and human beings bear witness to that by their deeds;
they love wealth too much.
Don't they know
that when the graves are opened,
and that which is within hearts is revealed,
it will be clear what their Sustainer was well-aware of all along?

[100:1-11]

The Day of Astonishment

ʾAl-Qāriʿah

The Day of Astonishment:
What is the Day of Astonishment?
And what will explain to you what the Day of Astonishment is?
It is a Day when human beings will be like scattered moths
and the mountains will be like fluffs of wool.
Then those whose balance is heavy with good deeds
will find themselves living in delight and contentment.
But the one whose balance is light
will find himself engulfed in an abyss.
What could make you understand what this would be?
A fiercely blazing fire.

[101:1-11]

Hoarding

ʾAt-Takāthur

Competition in hoarding distracts you
until you journey to the graves.
But you shall soon know the reality.
Again, you will soon know.

[102:1-4]

Time

ʾAl-ʿAṣr

In the Name of God,
the Infinitely Compassionate and Most Merciful
Consider time . . . .
Truly, human beings are in loss
except those who have faith and do righteous deeds
and encourage each other in the teaching of Truth
and of patient perseverance.

Bismillāhir Raḥmānir Raḥeem
Wal ʿaṣri
ʾIn nal innsāna lafi khusrin
ʾIllal lazhīna ʾāmanū wa ʿamiluṣ ṣāliḥāti
wa tawāṣaw bil ḥaqqi wa tawāṣaw biṣ ṣabr.

بِسْمِ اللَّهِ الرَّحْمَٰنِ الرَّحِيمِ
وَٱلْعَصْرِ ۝ إِنَّ ٱلْإِنسَٰنَ لَفِى خُسْرٍ ۝ إِلَّا ٱلَّذِينَ ءَامَنُوا۟
وَعَمِلُوا۟ ٱلصَّٰلِحَٰتِ وَتَوَاصَوْا۟ بِٱلْحَقِّ وَتَوَاصَوْا۟ بِٱلصَّبْرِ ۝

[103:1-3]

The Slanderer

ʾAl-Humazah

Grief to all those who spread scandal, speaking ill of others;
those who amass wealth and hoard it,
thinking that wealth could make them immortal!
By no means!
They will be sure to be thrown into that which breaks to pieces.
And what will explain to you "that which breaks to pieces?"—
the fire kindled by God which overwhelms hearts:[76]
it shall arch over them in broad reaching columns.

[104:1-9]

The Elephant

ʾAl-Fīl

Don't you see how your Sustainer
dealt with the Companions of the Elephant?[77]
Didn't He thwart their treacherous plan?
And He sent against them swarms of birds
striking them with stones of baked clay.
Then He caused them to become like a field of grain reduced to stubble.

[105:1-5]

---

[76]I.e., the emotional inferno that blazes in the hearts of those who focus on bettering themselves at the expense of others; ultimately, they are shattered by it.
[77]An army led by elephants approached Mecca and was miraculously defeated. This *surah* is an indication of the power of God to protect the "City of Security," or the heart of the human being, from apparently overwhelming forces.

The Quraish⁷⁸

Quraysh

In the Name of God, the Infinitely Compassionate and Most Merciful
For the bonds of security safeguarding the Quraish,
their safeguarding during journeys by winter and summer . . .
let them devote themselves to the Sustainer of this House,
Who provides them with food against hunger
and with security against fear.

[106:1-4]

Neighborly Needs

ʾAl-Māʿūn

In the Name of God, the Infinitely Compassionate and Most Merciful
Do you see the one who denies the Reckoning?
Such is one who shuns the orphan
and doesn't encourage the feeding of the poor.
So grief to the worshippers who do not pray with their hearts,
but only wish to be seen,
those who turn away from neighborly needs.

[107:1-7]

---

⁷⁸Custodians of the Kaʿbah, the tribe of Muhammad; ultimately, those who are of the faithful. The Kaʿbah, the Most Ancient Temple, is also a metaphor for the heart of the faithful one.

Abundance

Al-Kawthar[79]

In the Name of God,
the Infinitely Compassionate and Most Merciful
We have bestowed on you the source of abundance.
So to your Sustainer turn in prayer and sacrifice.
For the one who despises you will be cut off from all that is good.

Bismillāhir Raḥmānir Raḥeem
'Innaa 'aṭaynākal kawthar.
Faṣalli lirabbika wanḥar
'Inna shāni 'aka huwal 'abtarr.

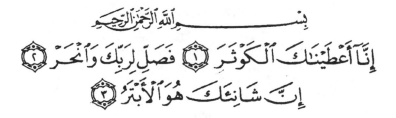

[108:1-3]

211

The Deniers

ʾAl-Kāfirūn

In the Name of God,
the Infinitely Compassionate and Most Merciful
Say: "O you who deny the Truth!
I do not worship that which you worship,
nor will you worship that which I worship.
And I will not worship that which you are used to worshipping,
nor will you worship that which I worship.
To you your Way and to me mine."

Bismillāhir Raḥmānir Raḥeem
Qul yaa ʾayuhal kāfiruun.
Laa ʾaʿbudu mā taʿbuduun.
Wa laa ʾantum ʿābidūna maa ʾaʿbud.
Wa laa ʾanā ʿābidum mā ʿabadtum.
Wa laa ʾantum ʿābidūna maa ʾaʿbud.
Lakum dīnukum wa liya deen.

[109:1-6]

Help

ʾAn-Naṣr

In the Name of God, the Infinitely Compassionate and Most Merciful
When the help of God comes and victory,
and you see people enter God's Way in crowds,
celebrate the praises of your Sustainer and pray for His forgiveness:
for He is Ever Turning One Towards Repentance.

Bismillāhir Raḥmānir Raḥeem
ʾIzhā jaaʾa naṣrullāhi wal fatḥ.
Wa ra ʾaytan nāsa yadkhulūna fī dīnillāhi ʾafwajaa.
Fasabbiḥ biḥamdi rabbika wastaghfirh.
ʾInnahū kāna tawwābaa.

[110:1-3]

The Twisted Strands

Al-Masad

Doomed are the hands of the Father of Flames![80] Doomed is he!
His wealth will be no use to him, nor any of his gains.
He will soon be burning in a blazing fire of flames,
his wife carrying wood, as fuel,
tied around her neck with twisted strands.

[111:2-5]

---

[80] Abu Lahab, Father of Flames, was the nickname given to Muhammad's unregenerate uncle, ʿAbd al-Uzza. He and his wife represent archetypes of those who spread the fire of hatred. Eventually the fire consumes them.

Purity

ʾAl-ʾIkhlāṣ

In the Name of God, the Infinitely Compassionate and Most Merciful
Say, "He is the One God;
God the Eternal Originator;
He does not bear children, nor was He born;
and He is beyond compare."

Bismillāhir Raḥmānir Raḥeem
Qul huwallāhu ʾaḥadd.
ʾAllāhuṣ ṣamadd.
Lam yalid wa lam yūlad.
Wa lam yakul lahū kufuwan ʾaḥadd.

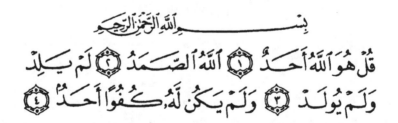

[112:1-4]

The Dawn

ʾAl-Falaq

In the Name of God, the Infinitely Compassionate and Most Merciful
Say, "I seek refuge with the Lord of the Dawn
from the mischief of created things;
from the evil of Darkness as it overspreads,
from the harmfulness of those who blow on knots;[81]
and from the harm of the envious one as he envies."

Bismillāhir Raḥmānir Raḥeem
Qul ʾaʿūzhu birabbil falaqq.
Min sharri mā khalaqq.
Wa min sharri ghāsiqin ʾizhā waqabb.
Wa min sharrin nafāthāti fil ʿuqadd.
Wa min sharri ḥāsidin ʾizhā ḥasadd.

بِسْمِ اللَّهِ الرَّحْمَٰنِ الرَّحِيمِ
قُلْ أَعُوذُ بِرَبِّ ٱلْفَلَقِ ﴿١﴾ مِن شَرِّ مَا خَلَقَ ﴿٢﴾ وَمِن
شَرِّ غَاسِقٍ إِذَا وَقَبَ ﴿٣﴾ وَمِن شَرِّ ٱلنَّفَّٰثَٰتِ فِى
ٱلْعُقَدِ ﴿٤﴾ وَمِن شَرِّ حَاسِدٍ إِذَا حَسَدَ ﴿٥﴾

[113:1-5]

---

[81] Those who cast spells; those who spread constriction, who exacerbate difficulties.

Humankind

An-Naas

In the Name of God, the Infinitely Compassionate and Most Merciful
Say, "I seek refuge with the Sustainer of humankind,
the Sovereign of humankind,
the God of humankind,
from the mischief of the slinking whisperer
who whispers in the hearts of human beings
among jinns and among humankind."

Bismillāhir Raḥmānir Raḥeem
Qul ʾaʿūzhu birabbin naas.
Malikin naas.
ʾIlāhin naas.
Min sharril waswāsil khannaas.
ʾAllazhī yuwaswisu fi ṣudūrin naas.
Minal jinnati wan naas.

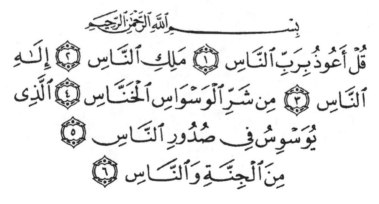

[114:1-6]

We have awakened
and all of creation has awakened for God,
Sustainer of all the worlds.
God, I ask You for the best the day has to offer,
opening, support, light, blessings, guidance,
and I seek refuge in You
from any harm in it and any harm that might come after it

~ Prayer of Muhammad

INDEX

Including References to the Ninety-Nine Names of God

221

بِسْمِ اللهِ الرَّحْمٰنِ الرَّحِيْمِ

اللهُ لَآ اِلٰهَ اِلَّا هُوَ الْحَيُّ الْقَيُّوْمُ لَا تَأْخُذُهُ سِنَةٌ وَّلَا نَوْمٌ لَهُ مَا فِى السَّمٰوٰتِ وَ مَا فِى الْاَرْضِ مَنْ ذَا الَّذِيْ يَشْفَعُ عِنْدَهُ اِلَّا بِاِذْنِهِ يَعْلَمُ مَا بَيْنَ اَيْدِيْهِمْ وَ مَا خَلْفَهُمْ وَلَا يُحِيْطُوْنَ بِشَيْءٍ مِّنْ عِلْمِهٖ اِلَّا بِمَا شَآءَ وَسِعَ كُرْسِيُّهُ السَّمٰوٰتِ وَالْاَرْضَ وَلَا يَئُوْدُهُ حِفْظُهُمَا وَهُوَ الْعَلِيُّ الْعَظِيْمُ ۝

[2:255]